Vintage Purses
At Their Best

Lynell K. Schwartz

With
Price
Guide

Schiffer Publishing Ltd

77 Lower Valley Road, Atglen, PA 19310

Dedication

This book is dedicated to the memory of
Margaret Sheehan Plouffe (Aunt Peggy),
who was a lovely lady and a teacher who
encouraged all children's creative talents
and to my young daughter
Lauren Lynell Schwartz,
whom I hope will grow to appreciate and
enjoy the wonderful old treasures the world
has to offer.

Printed in Hong Kong.
ISBN: 0-88740-831-1

Library of Congress Cataloging-in-Publication Data

Schwartz, Lynell K.
    Vintage purses: at their best/Lynell K.
Schwartz.
        p. cm.
    Includes bibliographical references and index.
    ISBN 0-88740-831-1
    1. Handbags--Collectors and collecting--United
States--Catalogs. I. Title.
NK4890.H34S38   1995
746.9'2--dc20   95-6380
                                             CIP

Published by Schiffer Publishing, Ltd.
77 Lower Valley Road
Atglen, PA 19310
Please write for a free catalog.
This book may be purchased from the publisher.
Please include $2.95 postage.
Try your bookstore first.

We are interested in hearing from authors
with book ideas on related subjects.

Acknowledgments

A very special "thank you" goes to
Cynthia L. Shulga of The Napier Company,
consulting historian Ann J. Chapdelaine,
Charles Whiting Rice formerly of The Whiting
& Davis Company, and Lyoda Orama of The
Napier Company. Thanks to photographer
and friend Dan Civitello for his patience and
Walter Kitik for his extensive photographic
contribution.

Also thanks to Bob Hogan, Eric Kitik,
and Bette Kitik for computer support, Carol
Schwartz for proofreading expertise, William
Schwartz for his artistry, proofreading, photography and general all-around support
and guidance, Susan Schwartz and Ruth and
Mills Mueser.

Thanks also to Carl Tunestam,
Stephanie Novell, Sharon Hall, Rosanna
Polizzotto, Diana Mercier and Bill Saunders.

My thanks go, as well, to Marie Kitik
for her support and enthusiasm. Thank you
to Filomena and William Swarzec for their un-
dying support and for the vehicle that helped
make it all possible.

My gratitude is extended to the fore-
most collectors in The United States for their
unwavering enthusiasm, support and for their
efforts in photographing their outstanding
purse collections and sharing them with all
of us, thereby allowing us to behold the very
best of vintage purses.

Contents

Introduction

As a dealer specializing in vintage purses, ladies' compacts, costume jewelry, and accessories, I have especially enjoyed my contacts with collectors and dealers who are eager to share their knowledge and experience so that together we are able to learn more about purses. From the home-spun styles to sophisticated imports to complicated mass-produced mesh, each purse has something to be appreciated. It is my hope that this book provides answers to some of the frequently asked questions and will be an interesting and useful reference to both novice and experienced collectors.

While conducting the research for this book, I was particularly impressed to discover the artistry behind the designs for mesh purses and the immeasurable work embroiderers and beadworkers put into the patterns in Victorian times. For some manufacturers, whose companies closed years ago, information is available only through the recollections of former employees or the persistent scanning of company documents. Each newly discovered vintage advertisement, trade card, and yellowing handbook became an important piece to a giant puzzle.

Finally, I offer a bit of advice to aspiring purse enthusiasts: if you love a purse and can afford it, you should buy it. What more pleasure can you gain than owning something that makes you happy? And for the merely practical-minded, the dramatic increase in value that purses have enjoyed over recent years may provide an indicator to future investment trends.

Art Forms in Glass Beads

In our own time the fashioning of beaded articles is not a fad; it is more than a love of adornment—it is artistry; there is a certain charm about the combining of colors which are made more beautiful by the play of light on the surface of the beads. We wish to leave you with this thought—that beadwork is always worthwhile; though fashion may change there is always a return to the beaded; the artistic work of your hands today will give you much satisfaction while the vogue is strong, and a work of art always lives, becoming enhanced by age in both value and sentiment.

Emma Post Barbour, 1924

Scenics

An open gate and curved pathway seem to give invitation for a park–like stroll. Thick looped fringe. 7 1/2x12. *From the Collection of Joyce Morgan, Photograph by Harry Barth*

Foreboding castles knitted in silk with minuscule beads are highly collectible. 8x12. *From the Collection of Joyce Morgan, Photograph by Harry Barth*

A popular floral scenic provides a vista through an open gateway. A lovely jeweled and enameled frame with colorful fringe add just the right touch. 8x12. *From the Collection of Joyce Morgan, Photograph by Harry Barth*

Fine beading of a house, lake and gazebo. Vandyke fringe in a lattice design, plunger top, turn of the century. 8x14. *From the Collection of Paula Higgins*

An unusual style of fringe and the unconventional usage of larger white beads combined with colorful fine beads are features that make this scenic stand out. 7 1/2x10. *From the Collection of Joyce Morgan, Photograph by Harry Barth*

Working women was a subject rarely depicted. This fine beaded autumnal scenic/figural of a woman gathering wood is noteworthy. 7 1/2x10. *From the Collection of Joyce Morgan, Photograph by Harry Barth*

Semi–fine glass beads were used to make this popular combination scene. 8x12 1/2. *From the Collection of Joyce Morgan, Photograph by Harry Barth*

Central medallion depicts a religious building or castle. Silver frame with a twist ball clasp. A gift to the collector, purchased in Scotland. European origin. 7x9 1/2. *From the Collection of Paula Higgins*

Tiny Venetian beads were used to make this bag. "Made in Italy" is sewn into the lining. 8x12. *From the Collection of Joyce Morgan, Photograph by Harry Barth*

Medium beaded castle scenic made on a loom, jeweled frame and carry chain. 7x9. *The Curiosity Shop*

A charming colorful garden with a jewel encrusted frame. 7x11. *From the Collection of Joyce Morgan, Photograph by Harry Barth*

Rarely seen is a bag with land transportation depicted. 8x10. *From the Collection of Joyce Morgan, Photograph by Harry Barth*

The combination of fine and semi–fine beads creates an unusual three–dimensional look. Realistic colors and innovative bead work beget a prize for the collection. It has a jeweled and enameled frame and complimentary twisted loop fringe. Early twentieth century. 7x10. *From the Collection of Madeline Hofer, Photograph by David Fowler*

A peaceful knitted scene of a cottage by a lake with a pair of swans. An added touch, metal swans attach the carry chain to the jeweled frame. 7 1/2x9 1/2. *From the Collection of Marion Held*

Swans flank an island. Fancy carry chain, extra thick fringe. 7 1/2x10. *From the Collection of Joyce Morgan, Photograph by Harry Barth*

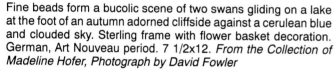

Fine beads form a bucolic scene of two swans gliding on a lake at the foot of an autumn adorned cliffside against a cerulean blue and clouded sky. Sterling frame with flower basket decoration. German, Art Nouveau period. 7 1/2x12. *From the Collection of Madeline Hofer, Photograph by David Fowler*

This delightful reticule demonstrates the historic transition of ships from sail to steam/sail by showing the traditional three masted warship with gunports in fine glass beads. It has the original linen lining. 6 1/2x7. *From the Collection of Paula Higgins*

The reverse side demonstrates a ship with three flying British flags, two masts with their sails unfurled, and a steam engine funnel with ribbons of smoke pouring from it, made in celebration of the monumental event that introduced the steam ship. *From the Collection of Paula Higgins*

Grapes, leaves and figures adorn the beautiful silver frame that tops a stylized castle scenic. 7x11. *From the Collection of Joyce Morgan, Photograph by Harry Barth*

A dainty sized scene of an early settler in front of a house nestled before a mountain. 6x9. *From the Collection of Joyce Morgan, Photograph by Walter Kitik*

This glorious castle courageously sits on the tip of the water in a remote mountainous area. Finely beaded, knitted. 7x10. From the *Collection of Marion Held*

An early plastic frame and carry chain is used on a floral/scenic combination. 6 1/2x10. *From the Collection of Joyce Morgan, Photograph by Harry Barth*

Medium bead loomed castle and moat scene. Simple straight fringe. 8x11. *The Curiosity Shop*

A pine tree shaded path leads to a house nestled in the woods. Silk taffeta lining, plunger top. European origin, early twentieth century. 7x10. *From the Collection of Paula Higgins*

Small beaded alpine scene reticule. 8x11. *From the Collection of Marion Held*

The classic castle scene in reticule form. 8x12. *From the Collection of Joyce Morgan, Photograph by Harry Barth*

An elaborate Taj Mahal style scene artistically executed in a realistic manner. 8x12. *From the Collection of Joyce Morgan, Photograph by Harry Barth*

Fine beaded scenics are hard to find in this small size. 3x4. *From the Collection of Fern Dengis, Photograph by Walter Kitik*

Reticules, Misers, and Tam-O-Shanters

An unusual subject, this Moorish figure rides atop a white steed toward a mausoleum. Palm trees in the distance lend a tropical flavor. Silk header, knitted, early nineteenth century. 6x10. *From the Collection of Paula Higgins*

The reverse side creatively depicts two court jesters in a covered boat somewhere in the tropics. *From the Collection of Paula Higgins*

This significant American reticule portrays a quaint mill in an oval medallion. Creators of bags like these boldly deviated from the more common three sectional floral and village scenic often made during this period. Silk crocheted header and drawstring. Early to mid-nineteenth century. 7 1/4x9 3/4. *From the Collection of Paula Higgins*

Three American early to mid-nineteenth century bags. Sterling frame, two with sawtooth borders and an unusual floral with green header. Approximate sizes: 5x8. *From the Collection of Paula Higgins*

A different artist's concept of the same subject. This knitted fine beaded reticule has a squared off bottom with loop fringe. Purchased in London, early to mid-nineteenth century. 6x8. *From the Collection of Marion Held*

Fine beaded floral with sectional depiction of the children's fable, "Mary had a little lamb." Silk header, extra long tassels, early nineteenth century. 8x10. *From the Collection of Marion Held*

A beautiful color scheme of American origin, with a linen lining. Knitted, early nineteenth century. 6x8. *From the Collection of Paula Higgins*

A cornucopia in rich pastels with a trailing rose motif typical of the early nineteenth century. Lovely hand whipped rings accommodate a silk pull cord. American origin, purchased in Williamsburg, Virginia. 6x7. *From the Collection of Paula Higgins*

Tulip shaped three sectional floral. Traditional sawtooth borders, hand whipped rings. Early nineteenth century. 6x8. *From the Collection of Paula Higgins*

Crystal color background beads behind a wildflower panorama, crocheted header with a drawstring cord, a tassel drops from the center of a beaded star design. Late nineteenth century. 7x9. Glass beaded, brightly colored Imari designed reticule with crocheted header and drawstring topped by quartz and finished with glass covered wooden beads. Late nineteenth century. 6 1/2x8. *From the Collection of Madeline Hofer, Photograph by David Fowler*

The Wellesley was a popular pattern during the Twenties. *The Hiawatha Book, 1924*

The Newport was made with Ebonoid beads that have optimal result when used with contrasting colors of silk thread. *The Hiawatha Book, 1924*

The Glossilla Blue Book of Bags and Ties, 1919

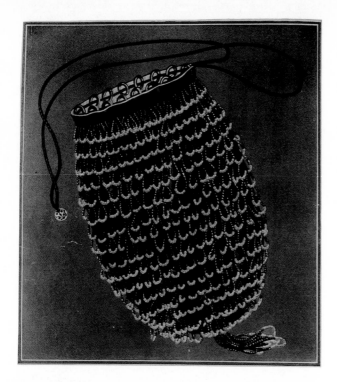

Rosebud Dewdrop was easily made and effective with small dark loops tipped with light colored beads, ca. 1924. *The New Bead Book*

This 1920s ladies' American college sorority bag finishes with a heavy tassel. 4x7. *From the Collection of Paula Higgins*

Green bead crocheted *Lady Gertrude*. Beaded ball accents at tips of carry cord, beaded tassel, ca. 1924. *The New Bead Book*

"Small, neat and necessary" is the Clover Mirror Tam-O-Shanter style wrist purse. *The Book of Bags, ca. 1920*

Bottom of Bag

No. 692

[26]

The *Miss Chicago*, a utility bag for the working woman of the 1920s with two views of a crocheted coin purse, ca. 1924. *The New Bead Book*

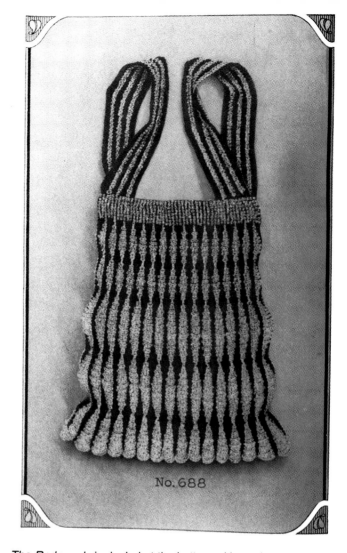

No. 688

The *Redmonde* is rippled at the bottom with graduated rows of crystal beads on garnet silk. *The Book of Bags, ca. 1920*

The "JEWEL"

Materials: 2 mass JULROBERTS Premier English Cut Beads, Size 8, Color No. 1.
1 mass JULROBERTS Premier English Cut Beads, Size 8, Color No. 2.
1 spool Purse Twist.
1 JULROBERTS Bag Cord, No. 57.
1 JULROBERTS Crochet Hook, No. 8.
Str. Col. No. 1 B.
1—Cr. 15 ch. st. without b. and join to form a ring.
2—Fill in with 28 whole st.
3—Cr. 2 ch. st. without b., then take 1 b. and cr. a h.st. in every other st. (3rd row contains 14 b.)
4—Inc. in each row until 10th row contains 60 b. in a circle.
5—Cr. 1 row, using Col. No. 2 B (60 b.)
6—Cr. 1 row loops Col. No. 1, using 8 b. to each loop.
7—Cr. 3 rows without b.
8—Cr. 1 row Col. No. 2 B., picking up with each b. the center of the loop to form a ridge.
Str. Beads for Design.
a—1 Col. No. 2 B, 5 Col. No. 1 B.   Repeat 10 more times.
b—2 Col. No. 2 B, 4 Col. No. 1 B.   Repeat 10 more times.
c—3 Col. No. 2 B, 3 Col. No. 1 B.   Repeat 10 more times.
d—2 Col. No. 2 B, 4 Col. No. 1 B.   Repeat 10 more times.
e—1 Col. No. 2 B, 5 Col. No. 1 B.   Repeat 10 more times.
Cr. all strung b.
Cr. same as rows 5 to 8 inclusive.
Str. Beads for 2nd Design.
f—Same as rows a, b, c. Repeat 10 more times.
g—4 Col. No. 2 B, 2 Col. No. 1 B.   Repeat 10 more times.
h—Same as rows c, b, a.
Cr. all strung B.
Cr. same as rows 5 to 8 inclusive.
Str. Beads for 3rd Design.
i—Same as rows a, b, c, d. Repeat 10 more times.
j—5 Col. No. 2 B, 1 Col. No. 1 B.   Repeat 10 more times.
k—Same as rows d, c, b, a.
Finish Bag with beaded scallop and sew on Bag Cord.

FOR FRINGE
Sew thread to bottom of Bag. Take 16 Col. No. 1 B. and 1 Col. No. 2 B. on the thread. On the 16th b. take needle back through the b. to bottom of bag which leaves a loop of 8 b. on the bottom of each string of the tassel. Make 8 strings for tassel.

Page Four

Purse making instructions for *The Jewel*, a popular 1920s reticule. *JulRoberts, 1925*

A pretty crocheted miser is shown with looped fringe beside a round bodied bag entitled, *La Vogue. The New Bead Book*

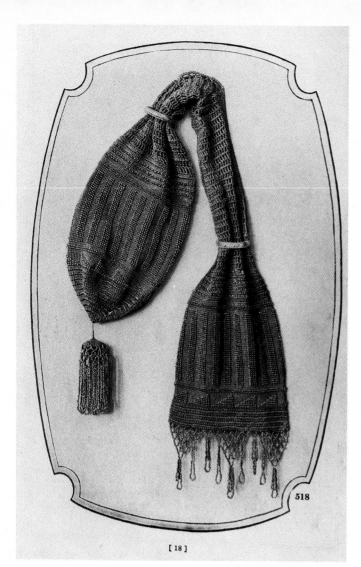

Materials—No. 666 Dk. Navy, 5 spools Hampton Crochet or 67 Cardinal Purse Twist. 8 bunches No. 8 Steel Beads. 1 button mold ⅝ in. in diameter. 1 Steel Crochet Needle No. 11. 1 spool Sewing Silk Cerise or Cardinal. 2 Steel Rings 1 in. diameter.

Round End of Bag—Ch. 4, join.

1st row—Ch. 3, 7 d. c. in ch. 4. **2nd row**—Ch. 3, 2 d. c. in each d. c. of previous row (14 d. c.), always sl. st. in top of ch. 3, at end of each row. **3rd row**—Ch. 3, 2 d. c. in each d. c. (28 d. c.). **4th row**—Ch. 3, * 1 d. c. in top of 1st d. c., 2 d. c. in top of next d. c., * repeat to end. **5th row**—Ch. 3, * 1 d. c. in top of 1st d. c., 1 d. c. in top of next d. c., 2 d. c. in next d. c., * repeat. **6th row**—Ch. 3, * 1 d. c. in each of 1st 3 d. c., 2 d. c. in next d. c., * repeat. **7th row**—Ch. 3, * 4 d. c. in each of 1st 4 d. c. of previous row, 2 d. c. in next d. c., * repeat. **8th row**—Ch. 3, * 5 d. c., 2 d. c. in next d. c., *. **9th row**—Ch. 3, * 6 d. c., 2 d. c. in next d. c., *. **10th row**—Ch. 3, * 7 d. c., 2 d. c. in next d. c., *. **11th row**—Ch. 3, * 8 d. c., 2 d. c. in next d. c., * repeat, break silk.

Beginning of Design—S. c. and bead (B.) rows are worked from wrong side of bag, when working take up one thread of silk only. Attach silk on which B. have been strung in top of ch. 3. **12th row**—* 1 s. c. with B., in top of 13 d. c., 1 s. c. without B., * repeat 9 times (there will be 10 groups of 13 B. and 1 s. c. without B. in this row). **13th row**—* 11 B., 3 s. c., * repeat 9 times. **14th row**—* 9 B., 5 s. c., * repeat 9 times. **15th row**—* 7 B., 7 s. c., * repeat 9 times. **16th row**—* 5 B., 9 s. c., * repeat 9 times. **17th row**—* 3 B., 11 s. c., * repeat 9 times. **18th row**—* 1 B., 13 s. c., * repeat 9 times. **19th row**—S. c. row. **20th and 21st rows**—B. rows. (Note—There are 140 sts. and as 144 sts. are necessary for pattern in upper part of bag, widen 4 times in 22nd row: work 34 s. c., 2 s. c. in next st. repeat to end.) **22nd and 23rd rows**—S. c. rows. **24th row**—* 4 B., 4 s. c., * repeat (there should be 18 groups of 4 B. and 4 s. c.). Repeat 24th row 36 times more. **61st and 62nd rows**—S. c. rows. **63rd and 64th rows**—B. rows. **65th and 66th rows**—S. c. rows. **67th row**—Ch. 3 (working on right side of bag), 1 d. c. in s. c. of previous row, * repeat. **68th row**—(Turn work) * 1 B., 1 s. c., * repeat. **69th row**—Same as 67th row. **70th row**—Same as 68th row. **71st row**—Same as 67th row. **72nd row**—Same as 68th row. **73rd row**—Same as 67th row. **74th row**—D. c. row. **75th row**—Ch. 4, 1 tr. c. (thread over needle twice) in 1st d. c. of previous row, * ch. 1, sk. 1 d. c., 1 tr. c. in next d. c., * repeat. **76th row**—Ch. 3 (turn work) 1 tr. c. between 1st 2 tr. c. of previous row, * ch. 1, 1 tr. c. in next mesh. * repeat to end. **77th, 78th and 79th rows**—Same as 76th row. Opening at sides of bag begins on next row. **80th row**—Ch. 4 (always count as 1 tr. c.), 1 tr. c. between 1st 2 tr. c. of previous row, ch. 1, 1 tr. c. in next m., 37 more tr. c. across row, turn. **81st row**—Ch. 4, between 1st and 2nd tr. c. of previous row for dec., ch. 4, 1 tr. c. in next m., repeat, turn. **82nd row**—Sl. st. in 1st m., ch. 4, 1 tr. c. in next m., ch. 1, 1 tr. c. in next m., repeat across row. Repeat 81st and

82nd rows 8 times more. At end of 97th row you have 21 tr. c. in row. This brings you to center of mesh section of bag. **98th row**—Ch. 4, 1 tr. c. in 1st m., ch. 1, 1 tr. c. in next m., repeat; 2 tr. c. in last m., always with "ch. 1" between for inc., turn. **99th row**—Ch. 4, 1 tr. c. in 1st m., ch. 1, 1 tr. c. in next m., repeat, ending with 2 tr. c. with ch. 1 between in last m. for inc., turn. 16 more tr. c. rows with inc. bring you to the closed end of bag. Attach your silk for the other half of m. section and repeat from 88th to 118th row, join to opposite half and work 5 more tr. c. rows same as 75th through 79th rows. **Next row**—* 1 d. c. on tr. c., 1 d. c. on m., * repeat across row (144 d. c.). **Next row**—D. c. on d. c. (slip on rings before proceeding with work.)

Square End of Bag—Beginning with 72nd row work backward through 12th row or the beginning row of triangular bead sections. Then 5 more rows of d. c., turn bag and sew ends together, always with care that the joining comes on sides of bag.

Fringe on Square End—Thread a bead needle with sewing silk having a double thread, attach it to bottom of bag at side, pick up 11 B., insert needle in bottom of bag about ¼ inch from side, this makes a little L., fasten securely and continue across bottom of bag (20 L. in all), at end of row run needle back through B. of 1st L. to the 6th B., then pick up 11 B., insert needle in 6th B. of next L., repeat until you have 5 L. in 2nd row, needle through to 6 B. of L. just made, then back 4 L. in next row, 3 L. in next, 2 L. in next and 1 L. in last row, pick up sufficient B. to make L. 1¼ inches long and fasten to center of L. Another L. 1 inch long and fasten securely in same place, break silk. Skip 7th L. on bottom of bag and starting with 8th L. make 2 more sections. Fasten silk between points and make 2 ch. L. 1¼ and 1 inches long in 7th loops, 1 L. in center of side points as shown in illustration.

Tassel for Round End—Cover for button mold as follows: Ch. 4, join in ring (R.). **1st row**—7 s. c. in R. **2nd row**—* 2 s. c. in next st., *. **3rd row**—* 2 s. c., 2 s. c. in next st., *. **4th row**—* 3 s. c., 2 s. c. in next st., *. **5th row**—* 4 s. c., 2 s. c. in next st., *. **6th row**—S. c. row. **7th row**—4 s. c., sk. 1, 1 s. c. in next st., 3 s. c., * repeat (insert button, rounded side up, and work under side to close). **8th row**—3 s. c., * sk. 1, 1 s. c. in next st., 2 s. c., *. **9th row**—2 s. c., * sk. 1 st., 1 s. c. in next st., 1 s. c., *. **10th row**—Sl. st. in 1st s. c., sk. 1 st., sl. st. in next st., repeat around button, close and break silk leaving about 9 inches, draw up through center of button and attach to bottom of bag. Thread needle with long double thread of sewing silk, attach to edge of button, pick up 11 B. and sk. 3 sts. on edge of button, insert needle and fasten silk, repeat around edge 11 more L. Run needle through 1st 6 B., pick up 11 B., catch in 6th B. of next L., repeat 2nd row same as 2nd row. Run needle through 1st L. on 3rd row to 6th B., 1 long L. of 90 B., catching in 6th B. again, run needle up other side of L. in intersection of 1st and 2nd L., down 2nd L. to 6th B., another L. of 90 B., continue until there are 12 long L. in all.

Directions for crocheting a miser called *The Sydney. A Book of Bags*, 1922

The floral motif characterizes this knitted miser as less common and more collectible. Purchase made in England. 2 1/2x8 l/2.
From the Collection of Marion Held

Figural

Exceptional fine beaded bag of a lady reading a book in a serene setting. Intricate enameled and jeweled frame. 8x12 1/2. *From the Collection of Joyce Morgan, Photograph by Harry Barth*

Renaissance couple depicted in fine and semi–fine Venetian beads with an intricate hand set mosaic frame. Frame incised "Made in Italy." 6 1/2x10. *Author's Collection, Photograph by Dan Civitello*

A gathering of party fanciers in a furnished room is unmatched in detail. 8x12 1/2. *From the Collection of Joyce Morgan, Photograph by Harry Barth*

Few beaded bags depict a scene in which the lady carries a purse. 7x9. *From the Collection of Joyce Morgan, Photograph by Harry Barth*

A charming young woman takes a dance in the garden. Gilt engraved and openworked frame with applied enameled tulips in fine beading. Made in Germany at the turn of the century. 7 1/2x10. *From the Collection of Madeline Hofer, Photograph by David Fowler*

This important American made bag features a compelling portrait of a black woman wearing a scarf and earrings made in the early to mid-nineteenth century. Handmade, possibly a self portrait, it was created with remnants made from materials similar to clothes that slaves wore, knitted with heavy dark beige silk, and a cut steel pattern on the reverse. The deteriorating beaded brown velvet strap demonstrates how well worn and cherished it must have been. 4 1/4x4 1/2. *From the Collection of Paula Higgins*

Scarce are beaded bags whose subject matter includes a black person like this interesting genie–like scene that tells a story only known by the purse maker. Mid to late nineteenth century. 5 1/2x7 1/2. *From the Collection of Joyce Morgan, Photograph by Harry Barth*

Grapes are depicted infrequently on beaded bags. This bag could have been made in Italy. 7x9 1/2. *From the Collection of Joyce Morgan, Photograph by Harry Barth*

Flower gardens were choice settings for scenes of romantic interludes. 5x9. *Author's Collection, Photograph by Dan Civitello*

The Butterfly Hunters. This knitted figural with a silver frame has unusual silver acorn drops. 9x10. *From the Collection of Marion Held*

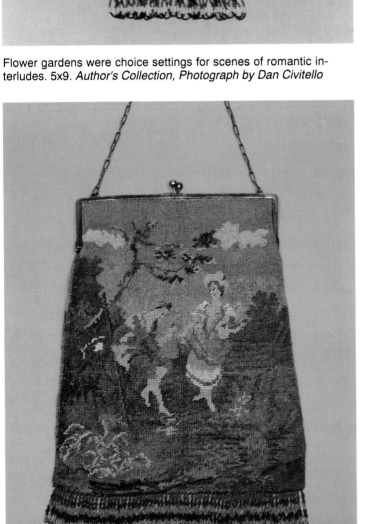

A bucolic scene of a romantic respite. 8x8 1/2. *From the Collection of Joyce Morgan, Photograph by Harry Barth*

The depiction of males on the reverse side makes the bag rare. *From the Collection of Marion Held*

A popular fine beaded figural design, *The Butterfly Hunters*, with a lovely gilt embossed glass jeweled purse frame. Late nineteenth century, European origin. 8x11. *From the Collection of Paula Higgins*

Early nineteenth century knitted reticule depicts children in different stages of play. A bell and sawtooth design with fine gold beading is used. Twisted loop fringe. 7x10. *From the Collection of Paula Higgins*

Close–up, children are shown with a ball, fifes and tambourines. Notice the early clothing they wear. *From the Collection of Paula Higgins*

Close-up, children playing with a wagon. *From the Collection of Paula Higgins*

A peasant couple seems to pray for a crop in a medium beaded scenic so extraordinarily done it has qualities indicative of a fine painting. The combination of lattice work and twisted loop fringe finishes the bag in a grand way. 6x8 1/2. *From the Collection of Joyce Morgan, Photograph by Harry Barth*

A romantic Renaissance couple with a basket of roses at their feet. Sterling embossed frame. 7x10. *Author's Collection, Photograph by Dan Civitello*

A couple enjoys a romantic dance while a musician entertains with a flute. 7x7 1/2. *From the Collection of Marion Held*

Three sectional knitted bag of a brave cavalier amid a gazebo and trees. Sawtooth design from the mid-nineteenth century. 6 1/4x8 3/4. *From the Collection of Paula Higgins*

Austrian fine beaded scenic depicting the serenading of a sweetheart. 5x8. *Author's Collection, Photograph by Dan Civitello*

Hand knitted in Italy, a Renaissance depiction displays exceptional use of minuscule Venetian beads. 8x12. *Author's Collection, Photograph by Dan Civitello*

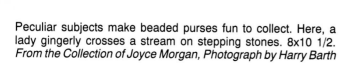

Made in Germany. 5x8. *From the Collection of Joyce Morgan, Photograph by Harry Barth*

Peculiar subjects make beaded purses fun to collect. Here, a lady gingerly crosses a stream on stepping stones. 8x10 1/2. *From the Collection of Joyce Morgan, Photograph by Harry Barth*

Florals

An unusual scalloped blue jeweled frame sets off the tiny blue flowers finely beaded in the body of the bag. 7x11. *From the Collection of Joyce Morgan, Photograph by Harry Barth*

Art Nouveau Satyrs gambol while cradling the gilt heavy sterling frame, their bellies adorned with ruby encrusted bands. Pearls, rubies and emeralds accentuate the frame that carries a fine beaded floral. The bag is finished with twisted loop fringe strung in colors depicted in the body of the bag. The plunger is crested with a ruby cabochon. Turn of the century. 9x13. *From the Collection of Paula Higgins*

Close-up view of the jeweled sterling frame with Satyrs allows us to observe the extra fine beading used. *From the Collection of Paula Higgins*

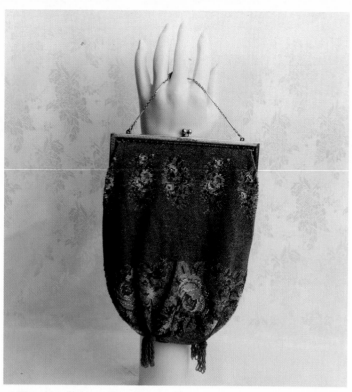

Fine beaded, sterling framed floral. Multiple tassels create an unusual finish. Turn of the century. 7x8. *From the Collection of Paula Higgins*

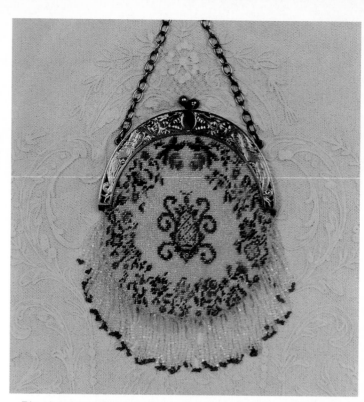

Pie shaped chatelaine bag incorporates opaque and metallic beads for effect. An incised sterling frame seems to roar with fiery dragons. Late nineteenth century. 5x7. *From the Collection of Madeline Hofer, Photograph by David Fowler*

A vase full of flowers is a subject not usually seen in floral motif bags. The design is done with such foresight that you can clearly see the stems through the water in the vase. Three sections of completely different flowers are depicted. Lattice style vandyke fringe finishes with a loop. 8x12. *From the Collection of Joyce Morgan, Photograph by Harry Barth*

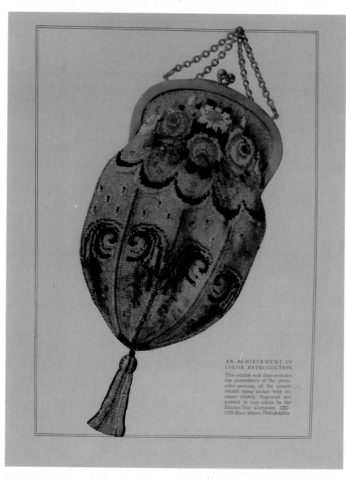

This lovely floral bag was advertised not for the bag itself, but instead, to show color reproduction! Ca. 1917. *Theatre Magazine*

Stylized lilies in medium beads, Belgium. Early twentieth century. 6x9. *From the Collection of Paula Higgins*

Popular floral with fine glass beads forming a garland with blue bell shaped flowers. The elaborately embossed gilt over brass frame and carry chain is accented with lapis lazuli and faux sapphires. Metal swans connecting the frame to the carry chain and a flower basket pendant drop contribute to its charm. 7 1/2x11. *From the Collection of Madeline Hofer, Photograph by David Fowler*

An extra large bag. 9x13. *From the Collection of Joyce Morgan, Photograph by Harry Barth*

Close–up. *From the Collection of Madeline Hofer, Photograph by David Fowler*

Twin cabbage roses are centered in the heavily beaded floral against a black and white background. Hand engraved silver frame, loop fringe. 5x10. Three large roses are the subject of the bag with the large 800 silver frame that has dancing figures and amusing squirrels affixed to the frame to hold the carry chain. 8x13. *From the Collection of Paula Higgins*

An intricate all–over floral pattern constructed with fine glass beads. Gilt over brass embossed and openworked frame with applied enamel decoration, silk lining with original kid lined coin purse. 7x11. *From the Collection of Madeline Hofer, Photograph by David Fowler*

The original label sewn inside the bag reads, "Cecile." 7x10. *From the Collection of Joyce Morgan, Photograph by Harry Barth*

Three faux cameos set this jeweled frame apart. Beads are fine grade and the bag is completed with a twisted loop fringe. 7x10. *From the Collection of Leslie Holms*

A crystal beaded background creates the perfect compliment to the triple rose medallion. The floral garland attractively adorns the bag just below the engraved brass frame. Lattice style vandyke fringe is tipped in loops. 8x12. *From the Collection of Madeline Hofer, Photograph by David Fowler*

The asymmetrical drawn net patterns at the center and three corners are key factors that make this lovely bag a novelty. Tiny opaque beads form flowers. Engraved brass frame, silk lining, tightly twisted loop fringe. 8x11. *From the Collection of Madeline Hofer, Photograph by David Fowler*

Fine beads and bold colors make up the reticule with a starburst of stylized flowers that measures 10x13 1/2. It has hand whipped rings and was made around the turn of the century. Medium beaded American scenic of a basket of flowers with an interesting double lattice work design measures 6x7. *From the Collection of Paula Higgins*

Swan's heads are curled to support the jeweled carry chain on the applied enamel frame that is set with three oval cabochons. 6x10. *From the Collection of Paula Higgins*

An all–over stylized design set against a vibrant pink background formulates a lovely effect on this medium beaded bag. Each design is outlined in black, finished with a simple loop fringe incorporating the colors used in the design of the purse. A twist ball clasp tops the gold embossed frame. 1920s. 7x11. *From the Collection of Paula Higgins*

Art Deco inspired floral with fine beading in an abstract design. The flaring toward the bottom of the purse was difficult to create. Silver engraved frame is in a diamond pattern, ca. 1920. 6x9. *From the Collection of Paula Higgins*

Exceptionally fine opaque and faceted glass beads combined with metallic beads lend dimension to this intricate all over flower design. Double hinged sterling engraved, openworked frame opens into the shape of a square. Elaborate vandyke fringe in a lattice design completes the purse. 8x15. *From the Collection of Madeline Hofer, Photograph by David Fowler*

American Indian-made in the nineteenth century, this quadruple tasseled bag was made with a combination of fine and medium beads on a heavy canvas and may have been made with intent to sell to the tourist trade. 6x7. *From the Collection of Paula Higgins*

The reverse side of the ornate mirror attached to the lining inside is a picture of a different, yet just as lovely, fine glass beaded floral. Perhaps another favorite purse of the original owner? *From the Collection of Paula Higgins*

"More than meets the eye," could be the title of this late nine-teenth century American fine beaded floral with a Greek key motif near the bottom. The inside attached mirror holds a surprise. 6x8 1/2. *From the Collection of Paula Higgins*

Daisy inspired American "over the arm" purse. 7x10. *From the Collection of Paula Higgins*

A beaded basket of flowers is topped with a wide Gothic style openworked frame encrusted with jewels. The frame, constructed of iron, is a medium used scarcely. Ball and socket clasp. Short twisted loop fringe forces the emphasis to be placed on the artistic wide frame with jeweled carry chain. 5 3/4x10. *From the Collection of Paula Higgins*

The Gothic iron frame shown open reveals the original beige silk taffeta lining with pocket. *From the Collection of Paula Higgins*

Detail is shown.

A delightful springtime scene of two robins on a cherry blossom branch. Nickel plating over white metal frame, inventive combination of large and small beads form the fringe, ca. 1910. 5x7 1/2. *From the Collection of Madeline Hofer, Photograph by David Fowler*

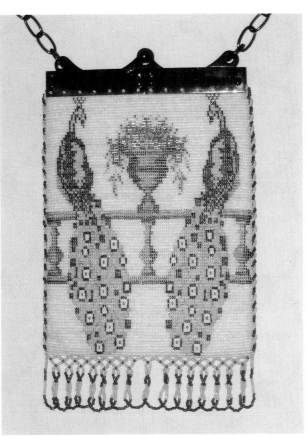

Vibrant twin peacocks in medium beads, faux tortoise shell frame and carry chain. 8 1/2x13 1/2. *From the Collection of Leslie Holms*

A strange combination of creatures with an unusual geometric border creates a one–of–a–kind collectible. 8x11. *From the Collection of Joyce Morgan, Photograph by Harry Barth*

Popular scene of a peacock perched on a branch. Heavy canvas with faux tortoise shell frame and carry chain. Ball and tassel fringe. This bag was found with a daguerreotype of a woman with child in "widows' weeds" that may have been an older relative of the original owner, ca. 1920. 6x9 1/2. *From the Collection of Paula Higgins*

An antelope, gazebo and trees are featured in this fine glass beaded reticule of the early nineteenth century. A multiple cornucopia motif graces the bottom of the bag and gray silk brocade lines this well maintained oldie. 5x7 1/2. *From the Collection of Paula Higgins*

This type of bird motif is routinely sewn on fabric. The distinct shape of the bag more commonly found in textile form, leads us to believe that the creator purposely transformed the style into beadwork. It is quite a treat to see one beaded, especially as nicely as this one is. 8x8. *From the Collection of Joyce Morgan, Photograph by Harry Barth*

Swags and Patterns

Multiple loops create this charming 1920s medium glass beaded wrist bag. The openworked filigree frame is made of silverplated white metal. 3x5 1/2. *From the Collection of Madeline Hofer, Photograph by David Fowler*

"A suggestion to increase your pleasure in the promenade." This glass beaded bag is entitled *The Boulevard*, ca. 1924. *The New Bead Book*

The Thames shown crocheted with large sized beads, below it, *The Sunshower,* was crocheted with medium sized glass beads and is connected to a bracelet ring. *A Charming Collection of Modern Beaded Bags, Hiawatha, 1924*

A pie-shaped bag called *The Rialto* above a common swag type called *The Sophomore. A Charming Collection of Modern Beaded Bags, Hiawatha, 1924*

The Niagara named for the cascading loops of "porcelain chalk beads" that drape from the bag. *A Charming Collection of Modern Beaded Bags, Hiawatha, 1924*

Usually a very common pattern, this swag adds interest with a fancy filigree frame combined with looped beads along the top and sides of the bag, *The Mandalay. A Charming Collection of Modern Beaded Bags, Hiawatha, 1924*

The *Fleur De Lis* was developed in beads from a classic motif, ca. 1924. *The New Bead Book*

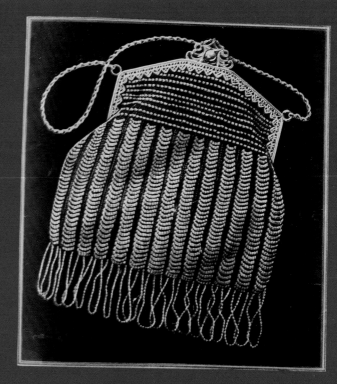

The *Matinee* is a charming bag for the afternoon, ca. 1924. *The New Bead Book*

"A smart bag of ample size which you will enjoy carrying" is *The Elizabethe*, ca. 1924. *The New Bead Book*

The *Chantilly* is pictured next to the geometric motif *Country Club. A Charming Collection of Modern Beaded Bags, Hiawatha, 1924*

Recommended for use with red transparent beads and grey silk is *The Fan–tan*, a common swag design with a pretty filigree frame. *A Charming Collection of Modern Beaded Bags, Hiawatha, 1924*

An imported French patterned evening bag made with tube shaped bugle beads sold for $1.00. It is pictured near a Dresden mesh purse. *Montgomery Ward, 1932*

Geometrics

A superior quality specimen of a European rug pattern purse with beads so tiny they can scarcely be detected with the naked eye. Thin sterling frames adorned these choice collectibles, made in the early twentieth century. 6 1/2x7 1/2. *From the Collection of Madeline Hofer, Photograph by David Fowler*

An exquisite example of a minutely beaded European made geometric with a carved jade elephant on the frame that slides to open. The sterling frame was most assuredly made by a famous silversmith company such as Unger or Gorham. Beige silk taffeta lining. 5 1/2x6. *From the Collection of Paula Higgins*

Early twentieth century rug pattern motif with ultra fine beads of European origin. A jewel encrusted and enameled frame adds the finishing touch. *From the Collection of Paula Higgins*

A detailed, intricate pattern in fine beads portrays yet another rug pattern motif. Pretty embossed frame, early twentieth century. 6x9. *From the Collection of Madeline Hofer, Photograph by David Fowler*

Extra fine beads are prevalent in a star shaped center rug motif. 8 1/2x12. *From the Collection of Joyce Morgan, Photograph by Harry Barth*

An Art Nouveau influenced, boldly colored, knitted rug motif pattern fine beaded bag. 9 1/2x9 1/2. *From the Collection of Marion Held*

This rounded bottom knitted geometric is composed of semi–fine beads, mid-nineteenth century. 6x8. *From the Collection of Paula Higgins*

An abstract design with an Indian flavor. 6x10. *From the Collection of Paula Higgins*

Early twentieth century abstract. 6x10. *From the Collection of Paula Higgins*

Fine beading in an oriental carpet design with an unusual color scheme. 7 1/2x10. *From the Collection of Paula Higgins*

Medium beads in star shapes match the embossing on the odd shaped frame. 3x4. *From the Collection of Joyce Morgan, Photograph by Harry Barth*

Intricate knitted rug motif/abstract pattern. Silk drawstring cord. 7x9. *From the Collection of Paula Higgins*

Extra long fringe lends distinction to this medium beaded paisley worked on net, turn-of-the-century. 6x10 1/2. *From the Collection of Paula Higgins*

Fine beaded oriental carpet design. 8x13. *From the Collection of Leslie Holms*

The Carmen displays a checkerboard pattern. *The Book of Bags, ca. 1920*

Regional Examples

Egyptian

Among the most greatly prized and sought-after purses available today are those with Egyptian motifs. Not many are still in existence now, although they were made in large quantity prior to and during the 1920s. In the late 1800s, exquisite silver examples of Egyptian motif chatelaines could be purchased in choice jewelry stores. The subject matter used in purse making was greatly affected by the frenzy brought on after the discovery of King Tutankhamun's tomb by Howard Carter in November of 1922. The young pharaoh had taken on the responsibility of the throne at approximately nine years of age in about 1334 B.C. During his reign, while still a child, he was married to Ankhesenamun, the daughter of Nafertiti who was famed to be the most beautiful woman in the world at that time. Tragically, King Tut died of unknown causes in his late teens and his grieving, loyal people gave him, what must be considered in the very least, an elaborate burial.

After spending almost thirty years in Egypt and nearly losing the financial backing of Lord Carnarvon, who had become discouraged after spending a small fortune on the project, Howard Carter finally experienced what he would later consider to be the best day of his life. On November 26, the archeologist drilled a hole into a door on the excavation site, large enough to accommodate a lighted candle, and he saw more riches than he had ever imagined.

Although the royal tomb's antechamber was in complete disarray due to careless thieves, the treasures, that later would be depicted on beaded purses such as magnificent statues, weapons and chariots, could be seen. Through the consuming darkness, ceremonial beds, thrones and the awe-inspiring glimmer of gold were detected. Carter concluded that the tomb had been robbed of some of its priceless gold and jewels not long after the king's burial.

On February 17, 1923, when the burial chamber was opened, members of the press and photographers from all over the world waited impatiently in the Egyptian sun, eager to bring news to their audiences. Enthusiasm had been mounting since the opening of the antechamber three months earlier. Designers and fashion experts were already creating jewelry, purses, and fashion accessories that mimicked the ancient artifacts so recently uncovered.

Once the pharaoh's coffin was excavated from the massive enclosure of the sarcophagus, and the body, encased in a solid gold inner coffin with a gold funerary mask covering the king's linen wrapped features was found, there was no stopping the popular furor that followed. Fashion fads followed this monumental event. Soon, leaders in the fashion industry in New York, London and Paris were designing bolts of cloth with a decided Egyptian influence. Celluloid powder containers for the dressing table had god-like images impressed into their lids. Jewelry and other accessories were created in the forms of scarabs; bracelets were made in gold and silver with plated shells of real beetles which were considered sacred by the ancient Egyptians. Screwback earrings were made extra long with golden images of The Sphinx set to dangle from the ears. Bauble rings carved from tiger–eye and lapis lazuli were made to emulate the pharaoh, cobras, and lotus blossoms, all of which had special significance to the ancient Egyptians.

The Egyptian style purses made in the 1920s were directly influenced by these events as, like wildfire, the designers were caught up in the intensity of this unique historical discovery. French celluloid frames were pressed to recreate the images of the ruler and his followers. Beaded and mesh bags depicted the lily of the Nile, the symbol of eternal life, pyramids, the sun god Ra, and the winged sun god Horus of Behdet. Pharaohs, the four protective goddesses with arms outstretched, the cobra and the vulture's head depicted on the headdress of royalty, and the great Sphinx of Gizeh, sculpted in the image of King Khephren with the body of a lion, now enhanced bags made during this period of Egyptian revival. Special symbols like hieroglyphics, the rising sun, messages of resurrection and eternal life that carried specific messages thousands of years ago, once again beckoned and were looked upon with great mystery and admiration.

Some bags influenced by this Egyptian discovery, usually depicting hieroglyphics, or stylized motifs, might be overlooked or termed to be geometric in design. If a purse does not contain a well-recognized Egyptian god or the famous Sphinx, it may unintentionally be passed up. Make no mistake, these bags are considered highly sought after collectibles. At any time, and especially in this particular instance, lack of recognition can be a costly mistake either by a collector or dealer. Even though some Egyptian motif bags were made with larger than tiny seed beads (or fine beads as they are called), their collectibility should not be disregarded. A bag may also be purchased for the value in the frame, whether it is made of celluloid, metal, or with glass jewels, but especially if it is greatly influenced by the discovery of King Tut's tomb.

Fine French metal beaded purse with a very detailed Egyptian scene of a pharaoh and a court musician. The top quarter of the bag contains hieroglyphics and the pendant drop is a pharaoh's head. The frame was made especially for this bag and carries a strong Egyptian influence that includes depictions of the vulture goddess, Nekhbet. 7 1/2x9 1/2. *From the Collection of Joyce Morgan, Photograph by Harry Barth*

French colored celluloid depiction of Cleopatra. Particulars include her headdress and long earrings. A simple black silk pouch leaves the emphasis on this exquisite wide frame, ca. 1920. 5x9. *From the Collection of Cindi St. Clair, Photograph by William Schwartz*

Artistic Egyptian motif chatelaines including E.A. Bliss wholesale catalog prices. *Courtesy of The Napier Company, Photograph by William Schwartz*

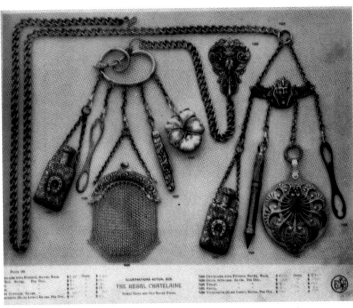

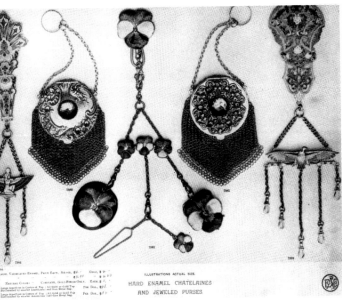

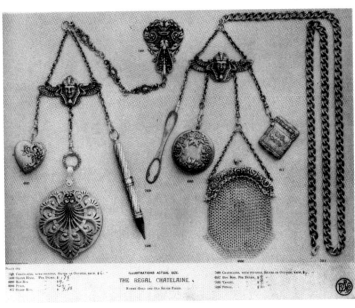

Cleopatra's head turns to the side to open the purse. *From the Collection of Cindi St. Clair*

Detail is shown in a rear view of the purse. *From the Collection of Cindi St. Clair*

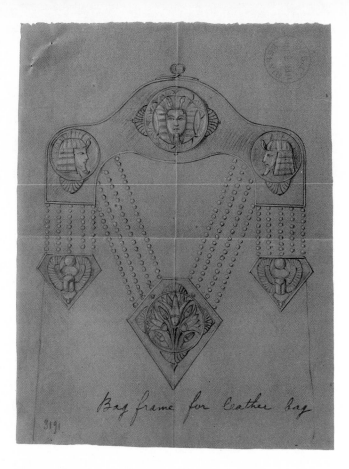

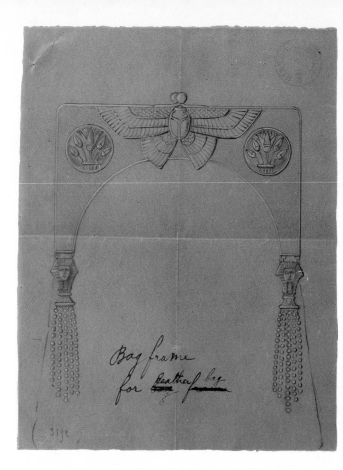

One of four French artist Egyptian design drawings. This lovely frame elaborately depicts a winged scarab with the body of a falcon symbolizing the sun along with lotus blossom and pharaoh's heads. It has a very uncommon decorative pendant drop, designed to be attached by rows of wired or strung beads. Affixed to the designs, written long ago, was the yellowed message: "Mr. W.E. Bliss asked Mr. Leroy for these for a special purpose." *Courtesy of The Napier Company*

Reverse side depicts a winged scarab and lotus blossoms. All of the Egyptian designs were created on July 5, 1911. *Courtesy of The Napier Company*

A large winged scarab, lotus, and small pharaoh's heads are the focus of this pretty frame, created to be used with a leather bag. *Courtesy of The Napier Company*

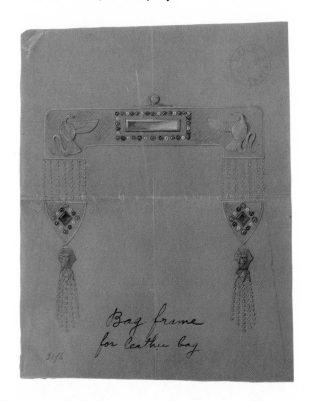

The reverse side depicts the vulture goddess, Nekhbet. Whether the Tiffany apprentice, Mr. William Rettenmeyer actually created these designs himself while employed as head of the design department remains a mystery. *Courtesy of The Napier Company*

Worked on with fine netted gauze, this medium beaded bag shows the Solar Disc, a winged scarab and lotus blossoms. The celluloid frame has stamped Egyptian figures. 8x10. *The Curiosity Shop*

Egyptian Sphinx motif celluloid encrusted with red beads, ca. 1920. 3 1/2x6. *From the Collection of Leslie Holms*

"The Egyptian" suggests the splendor of old Egypt in its design and coloring. A pair of phoenix birds is the focal point, ca. 1924. *The Bead Book*

A finely executed medium beaded pharaoh purse topped with a stylized celluloid sun for a frame. Colors are purposely chosen to depict the darker skin of the pharaoh with twisted loop fringe to match the colors in the bag. 8x11 1/2. *From the Collection of Joyce Morgan, Photograph by Harry Barth*

Scarab adorned openworked frame designed for The Bliss Company. December 26, 1911. *Courtesy of The Napier Company*

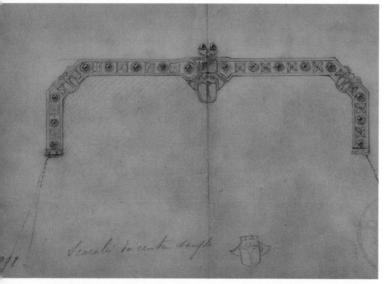

Lovely jeweled triple scarab motif. It is a rare treat to see the detailed pencil sketching of the scarab and French notations. August 19, 1912. *Courtesy of The Napier Company*

Three green marbled early plastic frames of the Egyptian Goddess Hathor measuring four inches across. Classified as "new" old store stock, they were in warehouse storage and not sold until recently, ca. 1920. *The Curiosity Shop, Photograph by Walter Kitik*

The Winged Disc of the Sun is flanked by the Sphinx. "GNS" is impressed inside the frame of this ring mesh purse. It has jewels in each corner and a jewel on the plunger top. 6x6 1/2. *From the Collection of Leslie Holms*

A fine glass beaded depiction of a kneeling pharaoh surrounded by the favorite flower of Egyptians, the lotus. 7x11. *From the Collection of Joyce Morgan, Photograph by Harry Barth*

An unusual depiction, ancient Egyptian sarcophagi are in each openworked area of the purse frame. October 25, 1911. *Courtesy of The Napier Company*

French cut steel reticule shown with two Egyptian motif purse frames, one in celluloid. 6x7. *The Curiosity Shop, Photograph by Walter Kitik*

Venetian

The ultimate preference of many connoisseur purse collectors is the Venetian scenic purse made with tiny glass beads, and they are the most difficult to find. Their scarcity, coupled with their appeal, creates a great challenge.

Since the twelfth century, the manufacture of beads for these special purses has been a regular industry in Venice, and in a number of European countries where people still engage in bead production. Unfortunately, these minuscule seed beads, or *perles*, as they are called, are no longer made. Their costly manufacture was slow and tedious.

The procedure began with skilled artisans collecting glass on a blow rod or iron into which another rod was inserted. Workers would stretch the glass by grasping one end and pulling it a distance of a hundred feet or more. The glass was then rough cut into smaller pieces by machine. The beads formed by this process were poured into a hopper filled with a slurry mixture. Here, they were smoothed by abrasive tumbling during a vibratory process similar to the effect on rocks finely polished by the ocean's waves. Next, they were placed in a furnace that slowly heated to approximately 700 degrees centigrade. Finally, they were precision ground, polished and sized. A fascinating variety of shades was achieved by melting colored glass in a large pot and adding aniline dyes or enamels. When the entire procedure was concluded, only about two pounds of beads were ready to be sold.

One of the means of promoting merchandise from Italy was the use of advertising trade cards which were given to storekeepers in hopes of creating a sale or, with luck, establishing a distributorship. The exporter G. Fabris introduced Venetian beads and fine beaded purses to Americans through the use of trade cards. These cards picture an extremely small beaded geometric reticule with twisted loop fringe, no doubt the merchant's finest bag at the time. The card attracted attention from prospective buyers whose first glance may have suggested that the purse was a decorative textile. This type of vintage advertisement is a vital link to the elusive history of purse importing. In fact, in the realm of purse collecting, even more difficult to find than the lovely Venetian motif bag itself is information pertaining to its history.

The Italian silversmith Coppini designed and created the 800 silver dolphin inspired purse frame that provides the ideal touch to this brightly colored ultra fine beaded Venetian water scene. 8x12. *Author's Collection, Photograph by Dan Civitello*

A rarely seen advertisement regarding exported European bags. The significant trade card offers Venetian beads and hand knitted beaded bags directly imported from an Italian merchant. *Photograph by Walter Kitik*

A tiny beaded reticule of a busy waterway in Italy. Tightly twisted loop fringe completes the bag. 8x12 1/2. *From the Collection of Leslie Holms*

A village under a romantic purple and blue evening sky. The artistic use of fine and extra fine beads adds dimension. A simple brass frame with a plunger top places emphasis on the bag. Late nineteenth century. 7x10 1/2. *From the Collection of Madeline Hofer, Photograph by David Fowler*

A detailed fine glass beaded Venetian street scene, unconventional because it does not include water. 7x10. *From the Collection of Joyce Morgan, Photograph by Harry Barth*

One of many artist's concepts of The Rialto Bridge across The Grand Canal from San Marcos Square. This lovely tiny glass beaded bag has a gold metal frame with blue jewels. Extra long interlocking twist fringe creates the ultimate finish, made in Italy in the mid- to late nineteenth century. 7x11. *From the Collection of Paula Higgins*

Seen through an elaborate Italian building, this fine beaded vista shows a gondola as it scans the darkened water of the canal in the evening. It has twisted loop fringe with a pendant drop in the same shape as the overhead light depicted in the building. 7 1/2x12 1/2. *From the Collection of Joyce Morgan, Photograph by Harry Barth*

Exquisitely worked Venetian scene of The Rialto Bridge and a gondola with exceptional use of very fine crystal and opaque beads that lend a dimensional effect. Gilt over brass embossed and jeweled frame with plunger top, made in Italy in the late nineteenth century. 5 1/2x9. *From the Collection of Madeline Hofer, Photograph by David Fowler*

49

A popular theme for Venetian scenes, this view of The Rialto Bridge and The Grand Canal enables us to see the bag with a different jeweled frame and color variations in beadwork. 5 1/2x9. *From the Collection of Joyce Morgan, Photograph by Harry Barth*

Exquisitely detailed village along the water's edge, which could be a Venetian scene. Charming flower basket carry chain connectors and pendant drop. 8x11 1/2. *From the Collection of Joyce Morgan, Photograph by Harry Barth*

A tiny glass beaded reticule of the popular Italian gondola skimming the water of The Grand Canal. 8x12. *From the Collection of Joyce Morgan, Photograph by Harry Barth*

Oriental

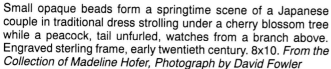

Small opaque beads form a springtime scene of a Japanese couple in traditional dress strolling under a cherry blossom tree while a peacock, tail unfurled, watches from a branch above. Engraved sterling frame, early twentieth century. 8x10. *From the Collection of Madeline Hofer, Photograph by David Fowler*

Set inside a scrolling red oriental style border is this fine beaded scenic that includes a Chinese junk on a waterway with a house and snow capped mountain in the background. Matching the colors in the beads is the beautiful and intricate mosaic frame, ca. 1900. 6x10 3/4. *From the Collection of Paula Higgins*

The floral motif mosaic frame shown up close is artistically pieced together with tiny shards of colored glass. *From the Collection of Paula Higgins*

A delightful depiction of an Oriental child with birds and flowers. A tiny glass beaded bag with brightly colored geometric borders. 7x11. *From the Collection of Joyce Morgan, Photograph by Harry Barth*

Fine glass beaded purse of a Japanese woman in a room that overlooks a garden. A detailed frame has a pendant drop that resembles an inverted fan. 8x9 1/2. *From the Collection of Joyce Morgan, Photograph by Harry Barth*

In traditional garb, this Oriental woman strolls along a stream. The enameled frame has faux pearls wired into a scalloped design. Notice the fine beaded border. 6x10. *From the Collection of Joyce Morgan, Photograph by Harry Barth*

An oriental building sits on the turbulent water's edge. Enameled daisies and cabochons adorn the frame. 6x8. *From the Collection of Joyce Morgan, Photograph by Harry Barth*

Fine glass beaded reticule. Crocheted header, early twentieth century. 7x12. *From the Collection of Joyce Morgan, Photograph by Harry Barth*

Ingenious Mesh

When thinking about collectible mesh bags, attention is usually directed to the popular mesh manufacturers of the Twenties and Thirties, namely Whiting and Davis, Mandalian and Napier. These companies have become well known through their persistent advertising. Other fine manufacturers include Evans, The R & G Company, and lesser-known European companies that also produced fine mesh purses.

Mesh was hardly a new material in the 1920s. In the Middle Ages, knights wore entire outfits including face masks, gloves and boots made of durable ring mesh for protection in battle. Long before that, ancient Egyptian and Greek soldiers were depicted wearing chain mail mesh. It is difficult now to determine when the first mesh purses were made, but early examples include the gun metal purses of the late 1700s.

Not until the nineteenth century did these bags increase in popularity among fashion conscious ladies. For all the thick petticoats, corsets, stylish hats and proper gloves, there was always room for one more compliment to an outfit—a perfect, shiny, little metal mesh purse! Designed to dangle from a chatelaine, wrist or pinkie, this accessory helped to make the lady a regal sight. Indeed, mesh had evolved from a material for protective garments to fashion luxury!

Chatelaine mesh purses were first popular in the 1800s. Usually made of German silver, plated silver, or gun metal, they had a ring in the center of the carry chain that could be attached to a chatelaine. Sometimes frames were very elaborate with castings or stampings of snakes, cherubs, and other figures. Later mesh purse frames showed ladies with flowing hair and flowers of an unmistakable Art Nouveau influence. Often, metal beads and elongated drops were attached to the bottom of the purse for adornment. The popularity of these bags continued through the turn of the twentieth century.

In the early twentieth century, a new style sterling mesh purse containing another smaller change purse connected as an integral part of the frame was available. This "two in one" novelty was not inexpensive to purchase. On the other hand, German silver and silver plated mesh bags sometimes were offered free to new subscription customers.

By the end of World War I, in 1918, life for female consumers became an exhilarating roller coaster ride into newly discovered emancipation. They had done their part, in as much as society allowed, for the benefit of the war by taking on traditionally male factory positions. As a result of the march and protest of the Suffragettes, the Nineteenth Amendment to the U. S. Constitution was passed on August 26, 1920, and women achieved the right to vote. This was the decade in which women's wear took a radical turn. Women began to wear bobbed hairdos, blazers and men's ties combined with long skirts. Gloves had taken a dramatic plunge in popularity leaving hands exposed, enhanced with rings. Long sleek gowns were accented with bracelets worn high on the arm. Showy metal headdresses were embellished with rhinestones or feathers. Black satin shoes flashed with sparkling cut steel buckles. Necklaces were extra long, sometimes past the knees, strung with imitation pearls and faceted glass beads. Flappers danced and partied to the early hours of the morning and smoked cigarettes in public. In this new lifestyle, ladies wanted a sturdy purse that was capable of holding their necessities: a hanky, their own money, a cigarette case, a tube of lipstick and a compact. Yet their wish was also for a delicate bag that could be worn over the wrist or arm without disrupting the flow of their hectic schedules.

The R & G Company enameled mesh bag with mirror inside. 3x7 1/2. *From the Collection of Joyce Morgan, Photograph by Harry Barth*

German silver flat mesh purse with "1902" stamped inside the Art Nouveau style frame. 4 3/4x7. *From the Collection of Paula Higgins*

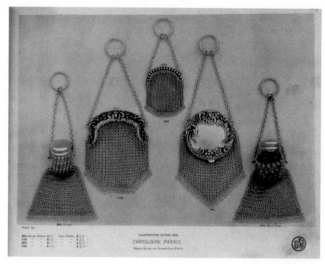

Chatelaine purses from The E.A. Bliss Company catalog. *Courtesy of The Napier Company archives*

"The latest Parisian creation— the regal chatelaine."

Courtesy of The Napier Company archives

Chatelaine armor mesh bag adorned with cherubs and flowers with many decorative drops. Marked "W & D sterling, 1918" on the frame. 4 1/2x6. *From the Collection of Madeline Hofer, Photograph by David Fowler*

Sterling finger ring purse with gate top frame. 2x3-3/4. *From the Collection of Paula Higgins*

Sterling ring mesh with engraved frame and attached change purse. 4 3/4x5. *From the Collection of Paula Higgins*

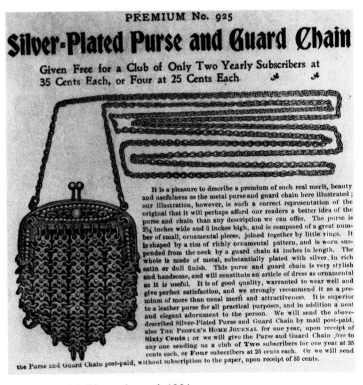

PREMIUM No. 925

Silver=Plated Purse and Guard Chain

Given Free for a Club of Only Two Yearly Subscribers at 35 Cents Each, or Four at 25 Cents Each.

It is a pleasure to describe a premium of such real merit, beauty and usefulness as the metal purse and guard chain here illustrated; our illustration, however, is such a correct representation of the original that it will perhaps afford our readers a better idea of the purse and chain than any description we can offer. The purse is 2¾ inches wide and 3 inches high, and is composed of a great number of small, ornamental pieces, joined together by little rings. It is shaped by a rim of richly ornamental pattern, and is worn suspended from the neck by a guard chain 44 inches in length. The whole is made of metal, substantially plated with silver, in rich satin or dull finish. This purse and guard chain is very stylish and handsome, and will constitute an article of dress as ornamental as it is useful. It is of good quality, warranted to wear well and give perfect satisfaction, and we strongly recommend it as a premium of more than usual merit and attractiveness. It is superior to a leather purse for all practical purposes, and in addition a neat and elegant adornment to the person. We will send the above-described Silver-Plated Purse and Guard Chain by mail post-paid, also THE PEOPLE'S HOME JOURNAL for one year, upon receipt of Sixty Cents; or we will give the Purse and Guard Chain *free* to any one sending us a club of **Two** subscribers for one year at 35 cents each, or **Four** subscribers at 25 cents each. Or we will send the Purse and Guard Chain post-paid, without subscription to the paper, upon receipt of 35 cents.

The People's Home Journal, 1901

55

GERMAN-SILVER MESH-BAG

Given for Ten Subscriptions

Premium No. 1256

EVER since the chain-mesh bags were first introduced, they have increased in popularity, and are now the most fashionable style to be seen. Jewelers get a fancy price for the same pattern we show here, yet every lady can earn one free by working for us. This is a **Guaranteed German-Silver, Ring Mesh-Bag**, lined with **White Kid** with extra change-pocket. The finish of frame is the popular and stylish **French Gray**. It is 5½ inches wide and 4½ inches deep, with a 14-inch chain. The picture plainly shows the richly embossed design of flowers and leaves which decorates the frame. In appearance and serviceability this Bag is a winner. We send it by mail prepaid.

SPECIAL OFFER If you will send us a club of ten subscriptions to this paper at our special Club-Raisers' price of **20 cents each**, we will send each subscriber this paper one year and we will send you a German-Silver Mesh-Bag (Premium No. 1256).

GOOD STORIES, Augusta, Maine

A free gift with ten subscriptions. *Good Stories, July 1913*

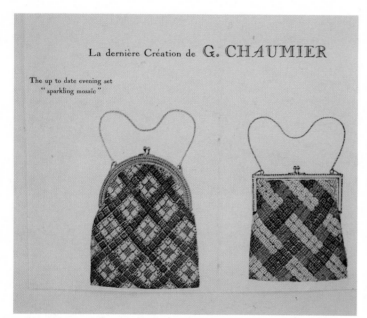

An advertisement for a pair of rare French mesh bags. *Courtesy of The Napier Company archives*

A unique jeweled ring mesh bag with attached brooch. It was made to be worn as a piece of jewelry on the shirt or at the waist. *Author's Collection, Photograph by Walter Kitik*

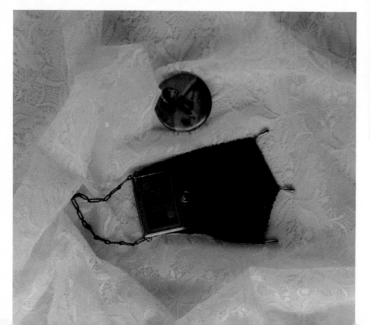

Art Deco French mesh bag with black and green enameled geometric design and tear drop fringe. 4x7. *The Curiosity Shop*

The respectable and dignified Edgerton Ames Bliss. Through this portrait taken in New York, he peers over the executive conference room at The Napier Company. *Courtesy of The Napier Company archives*

The E.A. Bliss Company as it appeared in 1901 after occupying the old flint glass factory. The flag stands at half mast in honor of the recent assassination of President William McKinley. *Courtesy of The Napier Company archives*

The Bliss/Napier Company was founded in 1875 when two men, a Mr. Whitney and a Mr. Rice, rented a small space in North Attleboro, Massachusetts to manufacture men's watch chains and small gifts. Their sales agent, Edgerton Ames Bliss, and a Mr. Carpenter agreed on a great future for jewelry and novelties so they purchased the company in 1882 and changed the company's name to Carpenter and Bliss. Soon it was evident that the thirty–three year old E.A. Bliss was the active head of the fledgling company. In July of that year, Mr. Carpenter retired and the company was incorporated as the E.A. Bliss Company. With a larger offering of goods and a New York office, Bliss, originally from New York State, traveled extensively to Europe to keep current on Parisian fashions. There he purchased stones and beads which he used to accentuate purse frames and manufacture jewelry. He possessed a high degree of business acumen and the company owed much of its early success to his untiring efforts.

In 1893, Bliss moved the main factory to an old ivy covered brick flint glass factory in Meriden, Connecticut that was one of the first ornamental glass producing plants in the country. Bliss hired William R. Rettenmeyer as the new chief designer and stylist. Rettenmeyer had apprenticed in silversmithing at Tiffany and Company and had studied designing at the Cooper Union in New York.

E.A. Bliss was the first company to manufacture sterling silver giftware and novelties in Meriden. Eventually, the city became known as *silver city* throughout the world, and the E.A. Bliss Company was considered one of the most prosperous in the area. Their product line was varied with jewelry and giftware including match safes, bonnet brushes, buckles, ornate manicure and stationary articles, fancy handled shoe horns and buttonhooks, lorgnettes, elaborate trays and lovely chatelaine purses. Launching an advertising campaign to reach quality retailers, they became a large supplier to fine jewelry and department stores. The fashion jewelry and accessories they offered grew in favor with the well–dressed gentlemen and ladies of the day. In the early 1900s, the New York office was moved to busy Fifth Avenue. Rettenmeyer's son Frederick joined the company in 1907. The company trademark during these early years consisted of "EA Co" in script with an imprint of a bee in flight above the letters, set inside a circle.

Chatelaine hooks of various designs were produced to coordinate with a selection of adornment fittings that could include vinaigrettes (a glass lined conceit that held aromatic vinegar, smelling salts and the like), scissors, bon bons (an ornamental flower or heart-shaped locket), writing tablets, combs and small purses. One type of chatelaine offered enamel decoration and another carried an Egyptian motif. Chatelaine purses and handkerchief pockets were of ring or armor-plate mesh, made from a variety of materials including white metal, gun metal, silver, and nickel silver. Many of these purses were lined with kid leather. Finishes on purse frames included French grey burnished, old silver and imitation gun metal. Mesh could be had in quadruple plate, silver, gun metal or glazed in Roman gold, bright silver, satin or old silver finishes. Ornate fittings could also be purchased separately. The wholesale cost of single chatelaine purses ranged from eighteen to forty–two dollars each. Bon bons were sold by the dozen for about ten dollars.

In 1911, at sixty–two years of age, Edgerton Bliss died suddenly at Magnolia, Massachusetts. Active in the company until the time of his death, he had spent the greater part of his life devoted to the development of the company bearing his name. His son, William E. Bliss, who was vice president of the company, became the active head soon after his father's death.

For a few short years beginning in 1911, exceptional designs of purses and purse frames were created with intent for production at Bliss. Unsigned by the originator, they were created on a special type of thin waxed paper that appears to have been folded in halves before being drawn to assure symmetry. Sketched, then tipped in color, they showed glorious detail incorporating gemstones, enameling, innovative shapes and originality. Some of the frames were meant to be cast from a mold, while others were designed to be stamped out on large presses. Many contained various penciled notations in French. Most included recent descriptive information such as: "Bag frame," or, interestingly enough, "From the Rue de la Paix." A few designs showed dimensions and pinpointed various parts such as unusual frame joints which needed added illustration to clarify the design. Occasionally, there were other sketches on the same page showing the bag from a more flattering angle and further describing its purpose and how it was to be worn. It is not known whether these unique pieces of artwork were made by the famed Tiffany apprentice Mr. Rettenmeyer who was employed at Bliss during this time. A curious document attached to four elaborate Egyptian motif designs stated the following: "E.A. Bliss asked Mr. Leroy for these for a special purpose." While a shroud of mystery still surrounds these rare pieces discovered in The Napier Company archives, it remains unknown whether these designs were manufactured or exist solely as archival drafts. Bliss must have foreseen their importance. Many were found precisely dated with red ink and stamped: "Received, Repair Department," or simply, "E.A. Bliss."

In the winter of 1913, William Rettenmeyer retired as head of the design department and his son, Frederick, took over his responsibilities. A year later, James H. Napier was hired as General Manager and Director. Under his direction, the company was revitalized with new personnel, machinery and products. Promotions and advertisements were increased as Napier instigated an immense period of development.

In 1919, the company introduced a fine mesh material called Nile–gold that was available with variations in the frame design. By advertising it in the trade publication *The Jeweler's Circular*, the company reached retail distributors who purchased in quantity. It was also advertised in the national publications *Vogue* and *The Red Book*. Bliss mesh bags included a complimentary silk pouch to be used in place of a lining. Along with the pouch came directions for the care of the bag with instructions for submitting it for repair service if needed.

The company trademark was changed again, this time to a rectangular block with the word "BLISS" inside. In 1920, Napier was elected President and General Manager. In recognition of his work in the growth and revitalization of the business, the name of the company was changed to The Napier–Bliss Company.

In the spring of 1921, the company introduced a vanity bag called the Du Barry bag with an innovative design that combined a mesh bag with a finely detailed and carved powder case that was attached to the mesh bag with a braided strap. The compact portion lay in the palm of the hand when carried and not in use. The Du Barry bag had a tassel on the bottom and an embossed frame in the shape of an inverted "V." It was available in 14 karat green gold, gold filled, sterling silver and Nile–gold. Two years later, Napier's contribution to the company was once again rewarded when the business name was changed to The Napier Company. In 1928, land and a large building on Cambridge Street in Meriden, Connecticut, was purchased and became known as Napier Park.

In the early 1940s, The Napier Company transformed its facilities to manufacture war-related materials. Among other items, radar panels, medals, metal bushings and millions of identification tags were produced. Highly skilled in precision work, brilliant designers and engineers developed a new process that conserved precious bronze at a time when metal supplies were critically low. Military items temporarily replaced jewelry, purses and accessories in the factory.

Over the years, The Napier Company continued to grow, opening sales offices in Chicago, Texas and Los Angeles. In 1960, James Napier died and Frederick Rettenmeyer was elected president. In the mid-Eighties, representatives such as Chairman of the Board John L. Shulga continued in the tradition set by Bliss by making European trips to purchase goods. The Napier Company continues to the present.

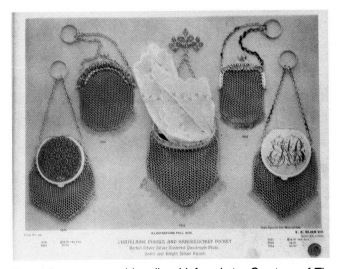

Chatelaine purses and handkerchief pockets. *Courtesy of The Napier Company archives*

One of many French artist design drawings created for The Bliss Company. It is not known whether these unique pieces of artwork were made by the famed Tiffany apprentice William Rettenmeyer who was employed as chief designer by the company during this time. *Courtesy of The Napier Company archives*

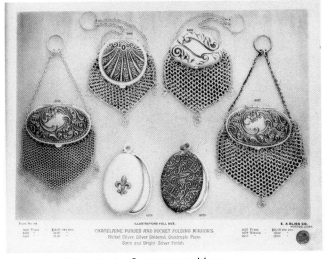

Courtesy of The Napier Company archives

A rare E.A. Bliss advertisement for a chatelaine bag. *Courtesy of The Napier Company archives*

Courtesy of The Napier Company archives

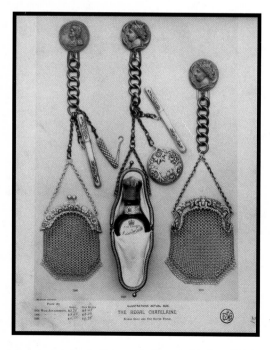

The regal chatelaine in Roman gold and old silver finishes. *Courtesy of The Napier Company archives*

Mr. and Mrs. Bliss as they appeared on an Atlantic City souvenir postcard. A fashionably dressed Mrs. Bliss holds one of her husband's latest mesh creations. *Courtesy of The Napier Company archives*

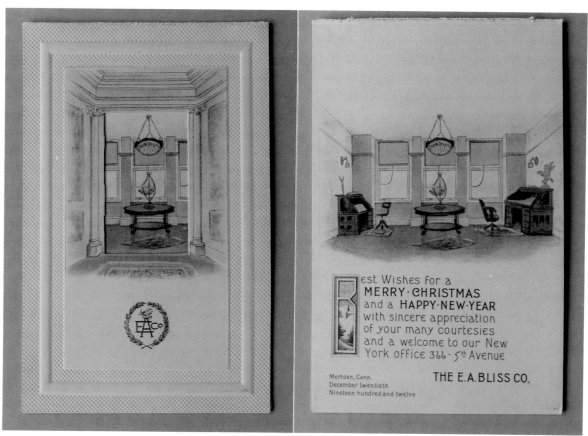

If you were a retailer or important customer of The E.A. Bliss Company in 1912, you would have received this expensive two–part holiday card. *Courtesy of The Napier Company archives*

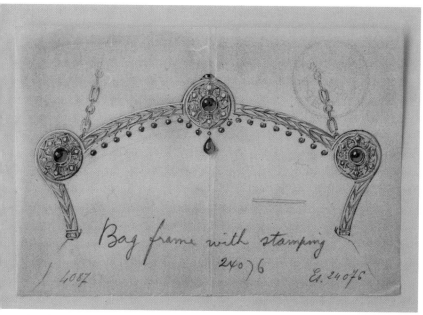

An elaborate frame that required machine stamping. October 2, 1912. *Courtesy of The Napier Company archives*

Dated: February 12, 1912, requiring machine stamping. *Courtesy of The Napier Company archives*

A thin mesh bag with a lock style clasp depicted at various perspectives. *Courtesy of The Napier Company archives*

A frame designed with a large opening. October 24, 1910. *Courtesy of The Napier Company archives*

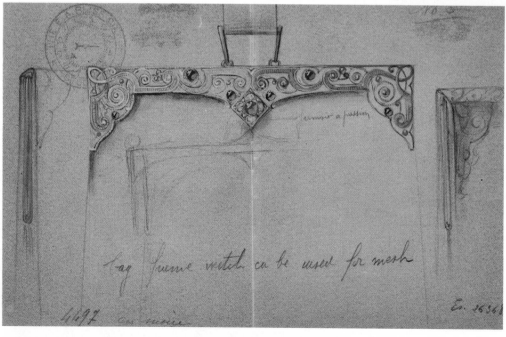

Designed to show two color variations with close–up views of hinge joints and critical areas. Notice the penciled French notations. May 13, 1913. *Courtesy of The Napier Company archives*

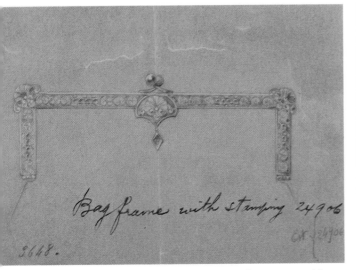

February 23, 1912. *Courtesy of The Napier Company archives*

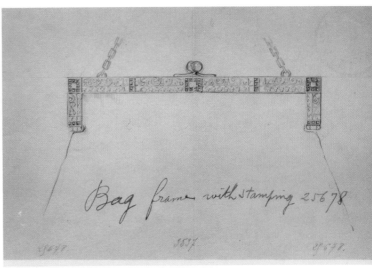

January 2, 1912. *Courtesy of The Napier Company archives*

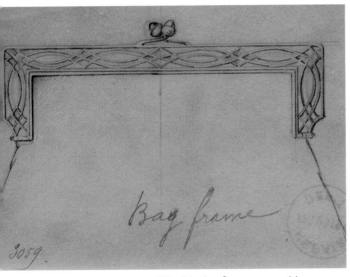

April 20, 1911. *Courtesy of The Napier Company archives*

December 26, 1911. *Courtesy of The Napier Company archives*

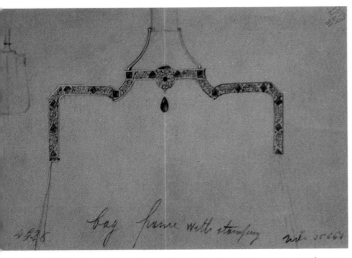

An additional sketch portrays the entire bag with an unusual carry strap. May 31, 1913. *Courtesy of The Napier Company archives*

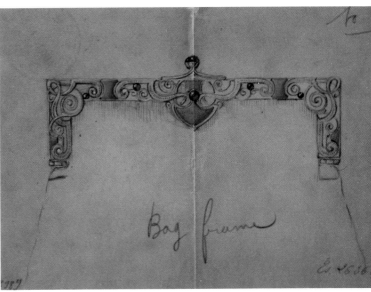

August 12, 1912. *Courtesy of The Napier Company archives*

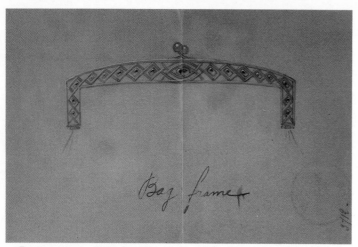

Pretty openwork design. March 21, 1912. *Courtesy of The Napier Company archives*

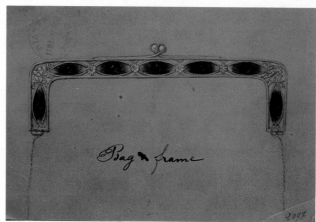

This design displays a complicated enameling technique. March 22, 1911. *Courtesy of The Napier Company archives*

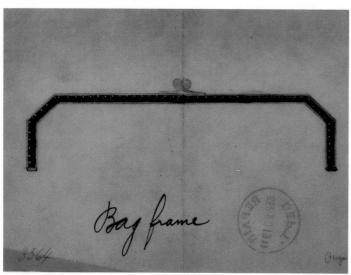

September 20, 1911. *Courtesy of The Napier Company archives*

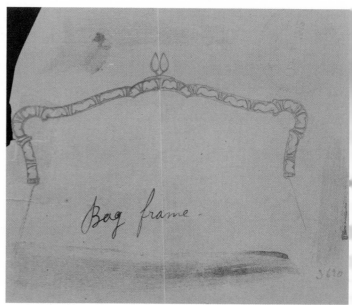

February 5, 1912. *Courtesy of The Napier Company archives*

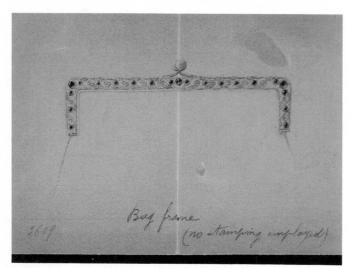

Designed to be cast from a mold. February 2, 1912. *Courtesy of The Napier Company archives*

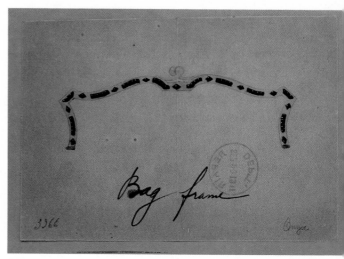

September 20, 1911. *Courtesy of The Napier Company archives*

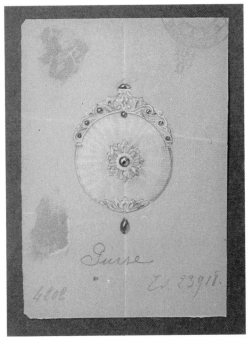

A small and elegant purse. December 12, 1912. *Courtesy of The Napier Company archives*

The intricacy of the design required the frame to be stamped on a press. *Courtesy of The Napier Company archives*

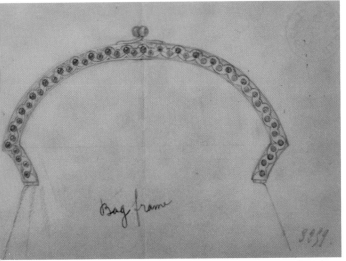

A design that suggests two slight variations in color and style. July 21, 1911. *Courtesy of The Napier Company archives*

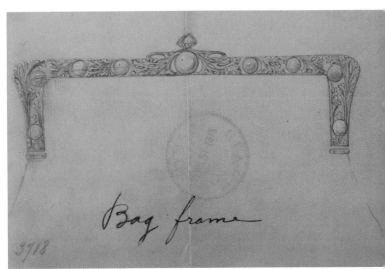

An intricate design with a funky fruit motif. March 21, 1912. *Courtesy of The Napier Company archives*

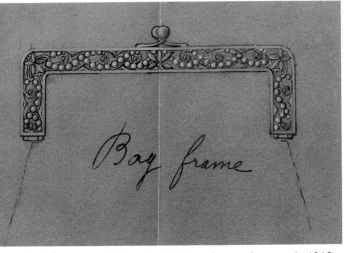

"Pearls" were probably wired into the frame. January 1, 1912. *Courtesy of The Napier Company archives*

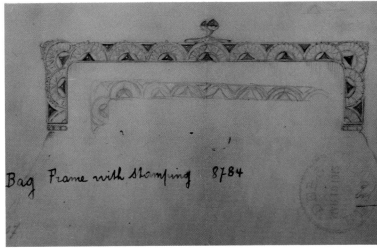

A non–cast frame with triangular shaped cabochon stones. March 19, 1912. *Courtesy of The Napier Company archives*

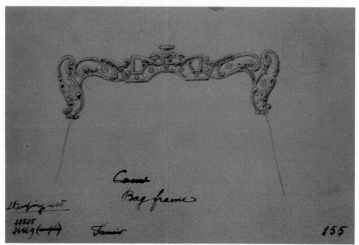

Highly decorative, created to be stamped by a press. November 2, 1910. *Courtesy of The Napier Company archives*

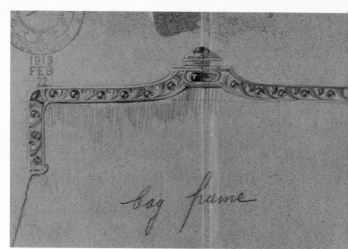

Displaying a highly decorative plunger top, this frame depicts two variations in color and design. February 22, 1913. *Courtesy of The Napier Company archives*

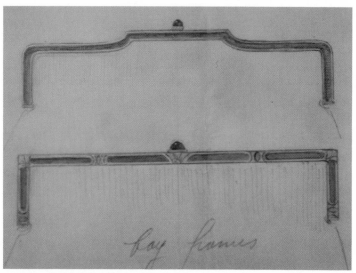

Two relatively simple designs. May 31, 1913. *Courtesy of The Napier Company archives*

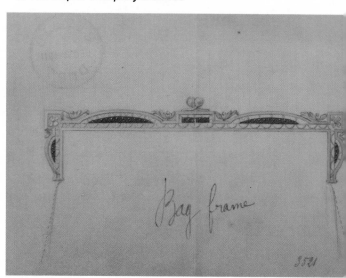

Special attention was given to the stones chosen for each design. December 20, 1911. *Courtesy of The Napier Company archives*

This frame is unusual because it attaches to metal trim shown to border the sides of the bag. *Courtesy of The Napier Company archives*

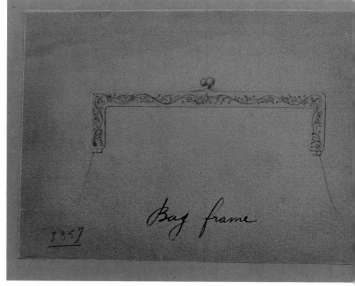

A delicate floral design. September 18, 1911. *Courtesy of The Napier Company archives*

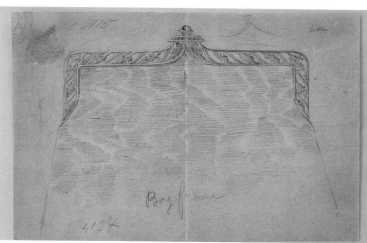

Beads were probably wired separately then attached to this intricate frame. *Courtesy of The Napier Company archives*

Two relatively simple designs. May 31, 1913. *Courtesy of The Napier Company archives*

A lovely maple leaf design with a jeweled plunger top. The body of the bag appears to be fine mesh in a geometric pattern that is similar to other French mesh purse designs. November 6, 1912. *Courtesy of The Napier Company archives*

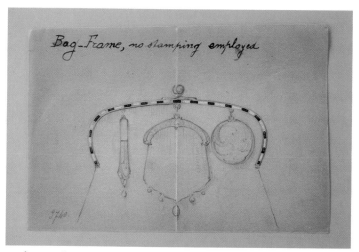

A rare glimpse of a complex interior that includes a coin purse, a locket or watch and an unidentified gadget. April 8, 1912. *Courtesy of The Napier Company archives*

A very elaborate and unique jeweled purse frame. The E.A. Bliss red inked stamp is clearly visible. Notice the unusual carry strap. February 12, 1913. *Courtesy of The Napier Company archives*

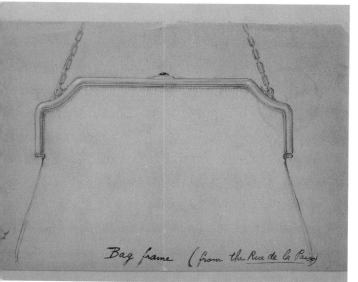

"From the Rue de la Paix." June 29, 1912. *Courtesy of The Napier Company archives*

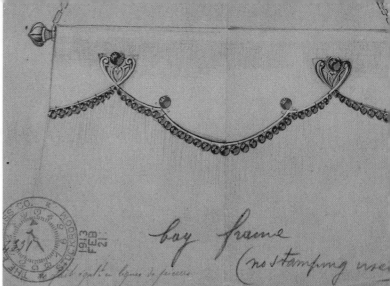

The elegant fold over style mesh bag is proof that a similar design was invented many years before Whiting and Davis's *Princess Mary*. February 21, 1913. *Courtesy of The Napier Company archives*

The scalloped interwoven frame design is the perfect complement to the vandyke style fringe shown with decorative bead drops. December 17, 1910. *Courtesy of The Napier Company archives*

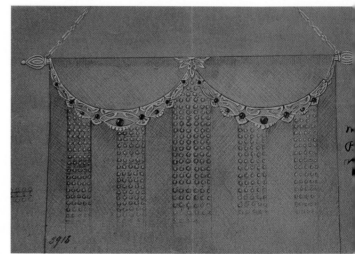

This unique fold over purse was designed to have faux jewels and pearls attached to the frame and mesh strips dangling from the frame in a grand style. *Courtesy of The Napier Company archives*

Beads are wired and draped through the stylish metal frame. A full view of the bag with a pleated skirt is depicted on the upper left. January 6, 1913. *Courtesy of The Napier Company archives*

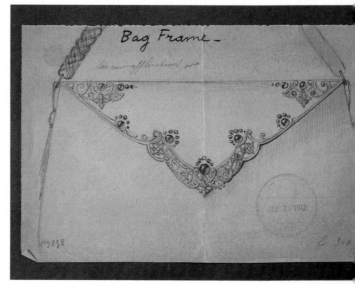

Ornate flap over purse with a braided carry chain. June 1, 1912. *Courtesy of The Napier Company archives*

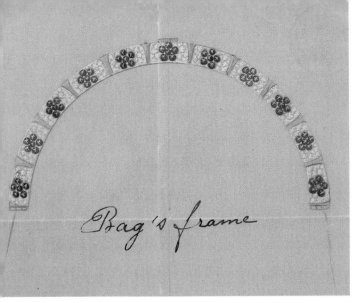

Substantially jeweled, arch-shaped floral frame. December 17 1910. *Courtesy of The Napier Company archives*

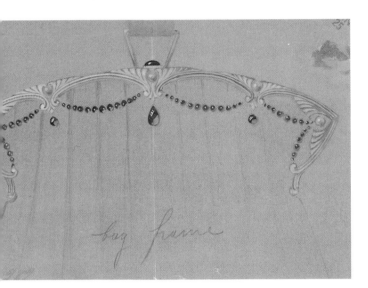

January 25, 1913. *Courtesy of The Napier Company archives*

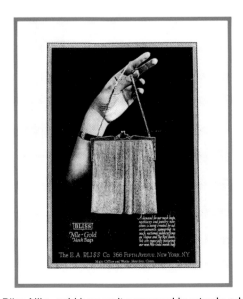

The Bliss Nile—gold bag as it appeared in a trade advertisement in 1919. *The Jeweler's Circular*

Bracelet ring purse with sketches of other perspectives. February 10, 1913. *Courtesy of The Napier Company archives*

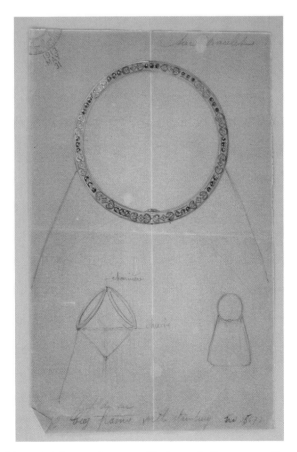

A bracelet ring mesh purse with views of other perspectives. May 31, 1913. *Courtesy of The Napier Company archives*

A small but expensive advertisement that appeared in *The New York Times* on December 6, 1931. *Courtesy of The Napier Company archives*

THE CARE OF YOUR MESH BAG

[BLISS]
The Mark of Quality

IF you take good care of your Bliss bag, you are assured of its long life. Never allow small change or pointed, sharp articles such as button-hooks, nail-files and the like to lie loose in your bag. Such articles should be put in the silk pouch enclosed in this package. The strain on the delicate mesh is thus greatly lessened.

If you should find it necessary to call our attention to the wear or service of your bag, return it to the factory with your name and address plainly written on a card and placed inside of the bag. Every consideration will be given it.

Not only shimmering mesh bags, but also snug little vanity boxes, curiously wrought chains and necklaces, delicately carved earrings and smart cigarette cases are shown in the irresistible Bliss Note Book. Write for a copy—free!

THE E. A. BLISS CO.
MERIDEN, CONN.

This onionskin paper outlining the care of the Bliss mesh bag and a silk pouch to be used as a lining, were gifts with a purchase. *Courtesy of The Napier Company archives*

A fine mesh Nile–gold bag. *The Curiosity Shop*

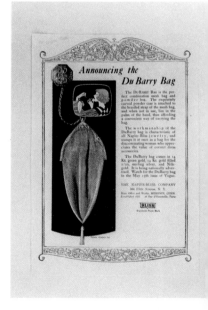

In the spring of 1921, Bliss intro-duced the *Du Barry Bag* with an in-novative vanity bag design that con-nected a carved powder box to the carry strap instead of a purse frame. *Courtesy of The Napier Company archives*

Courtesy of The Napier Company archives

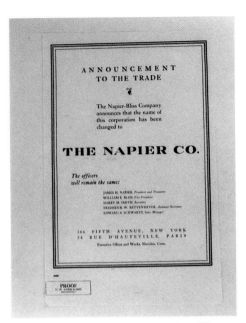

Fine mesh bags with "Napier" impressed into the frame's interior. The one on the left has an extra long carry chain, and measures 4x8, the other has a plunger top with a full skirt and measures 6x7. *Courtesy of The Napier Company archives*

Trade announcement outlining the Napier–Bliss name change. *The Jeweler's Circular*

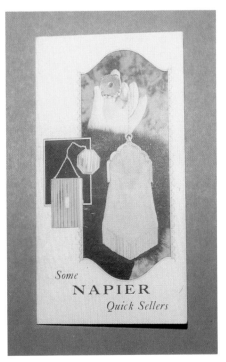

A vanity bag and vanity compact advertisement that appeared in a trade magazine, ca. 1920. *Courtesy of The Napier Company archives*

The factory as it looked shortly after the name change. *Courtesy of The Napier Company archives*

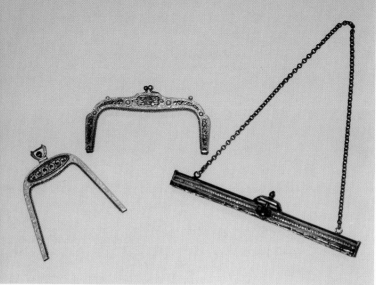

Three distinctly different Napier purse frames. The one on the right opens to form a square. *Courtesy of The Napier Company archives*

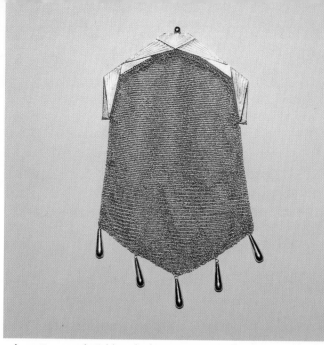

A pretty crosshatching design appears on the frame with elongated metal drops on the body of the bag. 4x6. *Courtesy of The Napier Company archives*

Napier sterling fine mesh purse with intricately embossed frame. Notice the extra long metal bars leading to the frame joints that afford the bag a wide opening. 3 1/2x5. *From the Collection of Joyce Morgan, Photograph by Harry Barth*

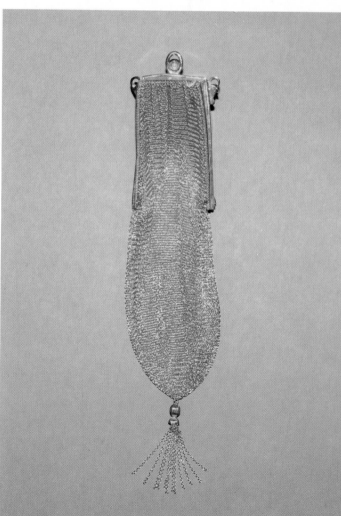

An exceptionally narrow bag with a large frame jaw reaching almost to the midway point in the bag. Not many finished with a tassel like this one. 2x7. *Courtesy of The Napier Company archives*

Charles A. Whiting, President and Treasurer of The Whiting and Davis Company, and the originator of the "modern" mesh bag.

The Wade Davis Company, founded in 1876 in Plainville, Massachusetts by William H. Wade and Edward P. Davis, manufactured jewelry. In 1880, one of the company office helpers was an ambitious teenager named Charles A. Whiting. Because of his enthusiasm and determination, this energetic young man was steadily promoted from his nine-cents-per-hour office position to New York sales manager. Remarkably, he became a partner in the company while still in his twenties. In 1896, he and Edward P. Davis formed a partnership and raised enough capital to purchase the company. Together, they changed the name to The Whiting & Davis Company and introduced the famous mesh bags. In 1907, Whiting purchased Davis's interest in the company and became President and Treasurer. He incorporated the business and, in a grand gesture, chose to continue with the name of the prospering company as a tribute to his longtime and loyal partner.

Demand for the mesh bags the company produced was steadily increasing. Made by hand, the work was meticulous. Whiting was acutely aware that a finished product ready for the marketplace took valuable time so he was eager to establish a faster, more efficient method of manufacturing the mesh. Accordingly, in 1912, he sought the aid of A.C. Pratt, the inventor of

Row after row of amazing mesh making mechanical spiders, able to magically transform a perfectly round column of silver into delicately woven and nearly transparent luminous thread at the rate of 700 links per minute.

the world's first automatic mesh machine. Whiting and Davis became the first company to use automatic mesh-making machineries that were soon rendered their exclusive property as they became the holders of the mesh making patents. The new reliable machinery increased the production of mesh bags tremendously. In conjunction with the growing volume, the company launched a major nationwide advertising campaign and became the world's leading mesh manufacturer. Aiming to reach the average family, and now able to keep costs down by producing in quantity, the company was capable of creating a fast selling, affordable product. Year round advertising was intensified just before graduation, Mother's Day, and the Holiday seasons.

By 1922, the Whiting & Davis Company had a branch factory in Quebec, Canada, a New York office on Fifth Avenue, and a Chicago branch besides their factory headquarters in Massachusetts. Their staff of fifty expert engineers and mechanics developed and registered numerous additional patents, and the company constructed nearly all the special machines used to make mesh right in their own plants. At Brown University, a study was conducted testing single rings of soldered mesh for tensile strength. Proudly, The Whiting & Davis Company reported that their minimum strength recorded was five pounds. The firm was the first to use solder–filled wire in making metal mesh. Three hundred and fifty highly automated mesh-making machines spun bars of solid metal into threads of gold and silver wire that were woven into many patterns and shapes of mesh. Links were made and woven with such quick precision that the process hummed along at the unbelievable rate of 600 to 700 rings per minute for each machine. If ever a single link was missed, or if the end of the spooled wire was reached, the machine automatically stopped until an attendant, who was in charge of up to fifteen machines at once, could remedy the problem.

A finished mesh purse might contain 100,000 links, each soldered individually. When the mesh was placed in an electric furnace, the thin trace of solder in each link melted and flowed. At first, the purses were joined to their frames with separate delicate links which were weakened when they were spread open. Later, the company introduced a fine spiral wire to join the mesh body to the frame. With the new spiral wire process one end could be freed and the whole spiral removed easily without opening a single link. This innovative method was called *hanging up*.

A *mesh to the edge* feature was another Whiting & Davis innovation that gave a smooth silhouette at the hinges and thereby added to the artistry of the purse. The Whiting & Davis logo was impressed into the metal purse frame and/or attached, with a small hanging metal tag, on the interior of the bag.

The Whiting & Davis Company guaranteed their purses' durability and dependability and supported their fine workmanship with a well–maintained service department in a special section of the plant. Under expert supervision, this department was a miniature factory in itself. No matter how roughly a bag was used, there was never a time when one could not be made as good as new either without charge or for a fraction of the original cost. In the service department, bags were taken apart and completely renewed. They were washed, polished and could even be replated if necessary. The company generously offered to repair other American-made mesh bags for a moderate fee. When they were reassembled to original specifications, usually within two to three weeks, they were sent back to their owners. It is intriguing to think that some of the existing bags may have been reconditioned by the specialists at Whiting & Davis.

Some of the styles of Whiting & Davis soldered and unsoldered mesh include Fine Ring Mesh (also known as Baby Ring Mesh), Sunset Mesh, and Fishscale Mesh. Sunset Mesh was available in various color combinations such as eighteen karat gold plate and silver plate in alternating gold, bronze and brass stripes. Fishscale Mesh was made from flat linked mesh with an attractive sheen.

A uniquely designed purse called The Princess Mary was made popular by Whiting & Davis. It had an envelope-shaped body and an interesting flap-over top. Constructed with a narrow frame that folded over a metal bar soldered to the sides, it was made in both large and small sizes as well as a dance version called The Princess Mary Dansant that consisted of an exterior coin purse attached to a regular-sized bag with a strap. Fashionably draped over the arm and adjusted by a mesh wrist strap, it offered little interference to the intricate moves of fancy dance stepping. The purse was named after the royal sister to Edward VIII and King George VI of England who, in a highly publicized wedding, married the sixth Earl of Harwood in 1922. The Princess Mary purse was also available in Sunset mesh style.

Purses early in the Twenties were made of sterling silver, 14 karat gold, 18 karat gold plate, and silver plate or gunmetal and had a fine silky texture, an almost-liquid suppleness. Since these purses did not have colored enamel, alluring designs were created with variations in frame shapes and embossing, with linked carry chains and mesh straps, and with a variety of unusual fringe that were given names such as Venetian, Egyptian and Bacchus. Especially ornate was the Venetian design that had a fleurette insert just above the fringe. Spanish influence prompted the use of metal fringe. In this decade, too, the free-flowing lines that emulated drapes of Classical Greek clothing were brought into vogue by The Whiting & Davis Company as they adapted these styles to mesh purse production.

During the Twenties, a splendid array of Dresden fine colored mesh purses was produced. Especially vibrant in color, these were made with a colored silk screened process which gave them a surrealistic, water-colored appearance. Fabulous enameled flat mesh purses known as Armor Mesh also were offered in varied colors and, when put into unusual patterns, the bags were well received. Single tiles or links were sometimes referred to as the *spider*. Links used to make the flat mesh bag consisted of a small piece of flat metal plate in the shape of a diamond with tiny "arms" at each point. The arms were used to connect with a small metal ring at each corner in order to create a flat surface. High speed presses punched out a large number of links and rings. They were individually woven into long sleeves of mesh fabric, then cut and sized. Another type of Armor Mesh was Beadlite that had a raised dot in the center of the spider giving the link a three-dimensional appearance. When enameled in color, it emulates beading. Whiting and Davis also sold El-Sah bags which had an additional metal tag attached on the inside and a stamp impressed into the frame. They were made from a variety of patterns and the El-Sah vanity bag is a treasure to find.

Whiting and Davis mesh purses were made in a constant parade of new patterns. Company representatives kept a constant vigil on the world of fashion in Paris and New York, thus enabling the company to anticipate major movements in the ever-changing modes of fashion. A noted french designer, Paul Poiret, gained world-wide attention when he banned the use of corsets in women's wear. Cleverly utilizing his celebrity status, he was paid substantial royalties for his contractual endorsement of the Parisian-inspired Whiting and Davis purse that carried his name in the mid-Twenties. Poiret Pouch Shape Costume Bags were made of Armor Mesh with silk lining and available in a variety of colors and could be acquired in exclusive jewelry shops. The most distinctive feature of the purse was its widened, pouch-shaped bottom. Advertisements for the purse emphasized its Parisian influence brought to the United States and included a colorful picture of Mr. Poiret who originated this new style.

The Art Deco style, which became popularized by the Exposition Internationale des Arts Decoratifs et Industriels Modernes in Paris in 1925, promoted a new look with geometric shapes and vivid colors that influenced designs of furniture, clothing, jewelry, and, of course, purses. Although its heyday was short lived, the style's influence can be seen throughout the subsequent decades. Because the economic prosperity of the

Main American Plant of WHITING & DAVIS COMPANY, Plainville, Norfolk County, Mass.
Canadian Plant, Sherbrooke, Quebec

The plant as it appeared in the early 1920s in Plainville, Massachusetts.

Naturalistic designs are depicted on these atypical Whiting and Davis enameled armor mesh bags. 4x6 1/2. *The Curiosity Shop, Photograph by Walter Kitik*

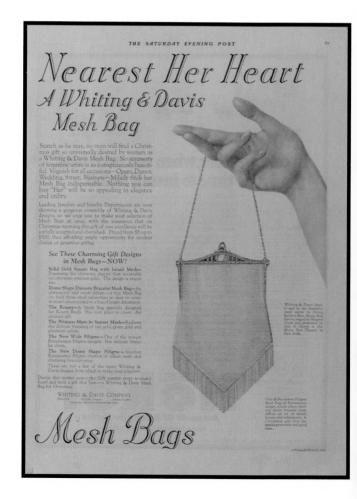

Whiting advertised extensively near the holidays. *The Saturday Evening Post, December 1923*

Twenties was eclipsed with the onset of The Great Depression in the Thirties, the purses produced by Whiting & Davis changed to accommodate more discerning customers.

In 1938, when Charles A. Whiting's grandson, Charles Whiting Rice, began working for the company, the new purses had already changed from colorful enameled mesh to solid gold- or silver-colors. Two years later, Charles A. Whiting died at seventy–six years of age, having been largely responsible for the business's success.

A few years before World War II, Whiting & Davis introduced a new style of mesh purse, the Alu–mesh. It was a white summer bag that sold for $4.95 to $7.95. Typically, frames were made of plastic and fabric tags with both the style name and the Whiting & Davis logo were sewn into the lining. During the peak year, 600,000 of these bags were made. Unfortunately, once purchased and used for the summer season, many were discarded.

From 1939 to 1945, new purse styles became simplified as practical clothes, shoes and accessories were the norms when the world was preoccupied with war. After 1945, the company continued to produce beautifully made purses in various styles using their famous mesh techniques. In 1966, the Whiting & Davis Company was sold to Certified Pharmaceuticals.

Today, The Whiting & Davis Company continues to produce mesh apparel and fashion accessories from the same type of materials including evening and day wear purses and purse accessories, and coin purses, wallets, checkbook covers, lipstick holders, and eyeglass cases. The fashion department has designed gowns, skirts and tops for celebrities such as Cher, Elizabeth Taylor, Morgan Fairchild, and Rita Moreno. Model Christie Brinkley was photographed draped in Whiting & Davis mesh for the cover of *Cosmopolitan* in September of 1983. Designer Michael Schmidt created a chain mail dress for Tina Turner in *Mad Max Beyond Thunderdome*. But, they also now produce other items for industrial use such as shark-proof diving suits, belts, and metal safety gloves for meat cutters. The company is preparing to move its factory headquarters to a new location in Massachusetts by 1995.

The Gift Enchanting

Radiantly beautiful as the happy Spring bride herself is the gift of a Whiting & Davis Mesh Bag. No gift can convey more delicately the esteem and exquisite taste of the giver.

Happy the bridesmaids, too, who receive a Whiting & Davis Mesh Bag to mark the momentous occasion. And the Bride of Yesterday, on her anniversary, thrills to the beauty imprisoned in shimmering silver or mellow gold. Doubly dear to feminine hearts for its smart correctness, as well as its daily usefulness.

WHITING & DAVIS COMPANY
Plainville (Norfolk County) Massachusetts
In Canada, Sherbrooke, Que.

Made in America—
Preferred by American Women

The Popular Whiting & Davis Renaissance Design

"Gifts That Last"

Whiting & Davis Mesh Bags
In the Better Grades. Made of the Famous Whiting Soldered Mesh

For the graduate. *Cosmopolitan, June 1923*

For the Spring bride. *The Designer, May 1924*

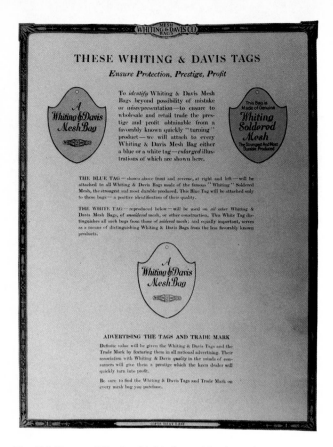

The Whiting and Davis shield-shaped trademark.

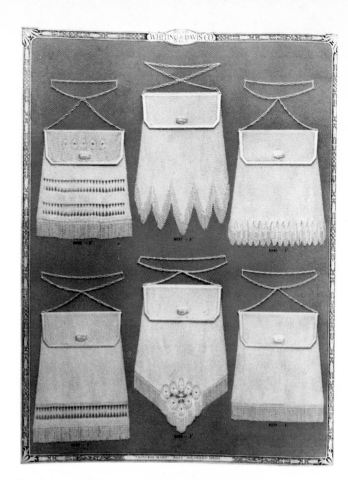

The *Princess Mary* baby soldered mesh, ca. 1922.

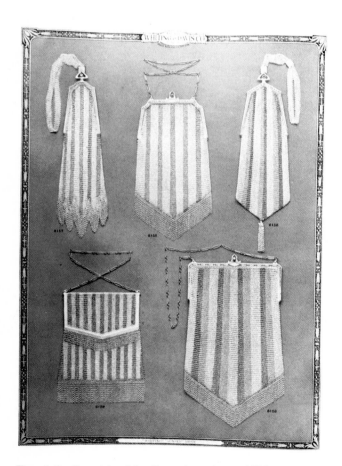

The distinctive style of the Sunset mesh, ca. 1922.

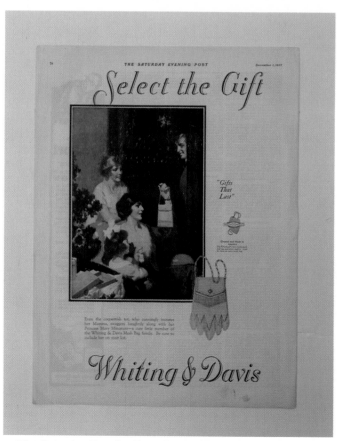

The Saturday Evening Post, December 1923

The famous flap over closure defines the *Princess Mary*. This one has a pretty fleurette insert called Venetian fringe. 5x7 1/2. *From the Collection of Paula Higgins*

A rare *Princess Mary* with enameled armor mesh and an enameled floral medallion. 4x4 1/2. *From the Collection of Joyce Morgan, Photograph by Harry Barth*

Solid 14 karat gold hand engraved designs, ca. 1922.

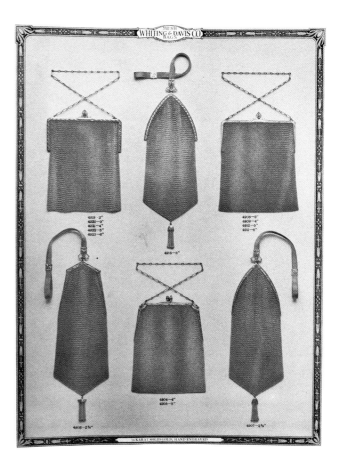

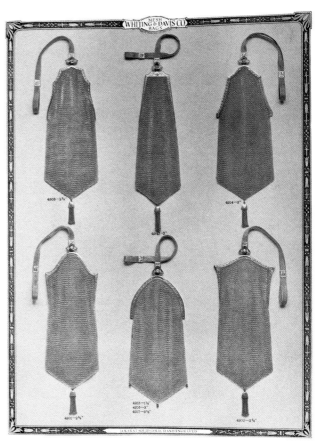

Sterling silver and hand engraved designs, ca. 1922.

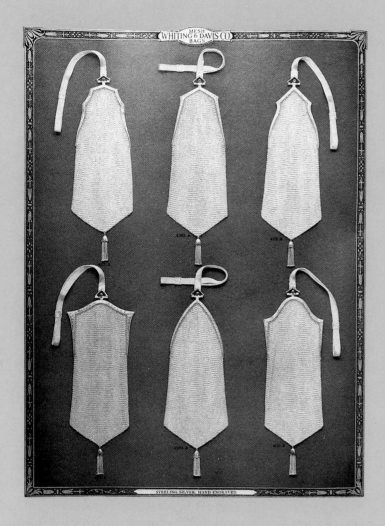

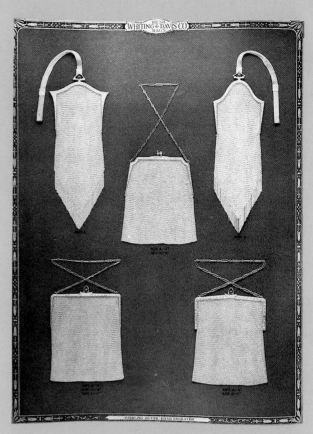

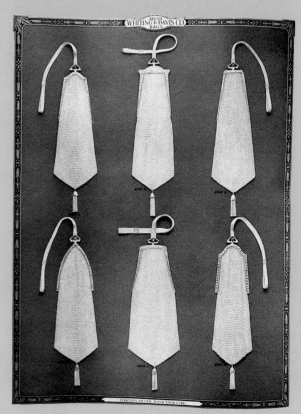

Styles in sterling silver including examples with hand engraving and very ornate fringe, ca. 1922.

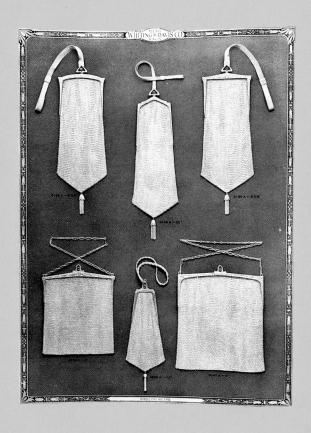

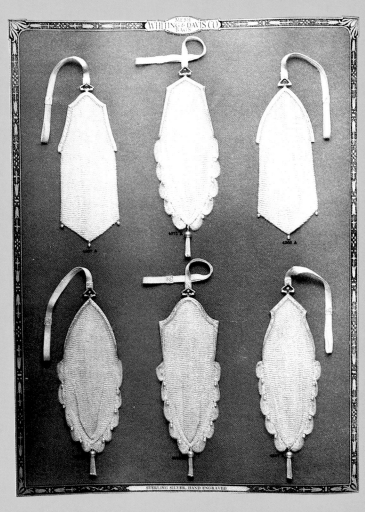

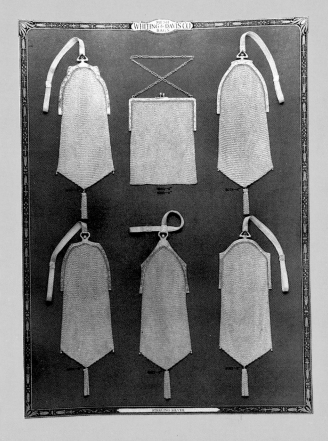

A trade advertisement that includes the Sunset mesh, the *Princess Mary*, and a vanity bag, ca. 1920s. *The Jeweler's Circular*

A displaying technique is introduced to retail distributors using The Wadco Easel. *The Jeweler's Circular*

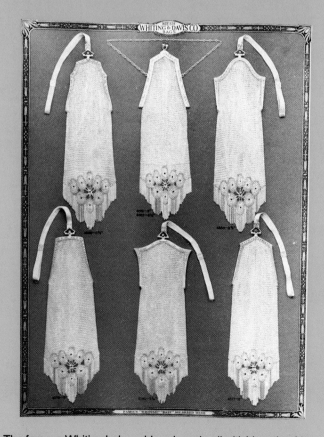

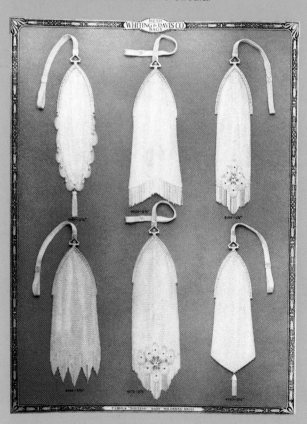

The famous Whiting baby soldered mesh, all with Venetian fringe.

Whiting baby soldered mesh. The lower left has Egyptian fringe, two have Venetian fringe.

Baby soldered mesh with a variety of fringe types, ca. 1922.

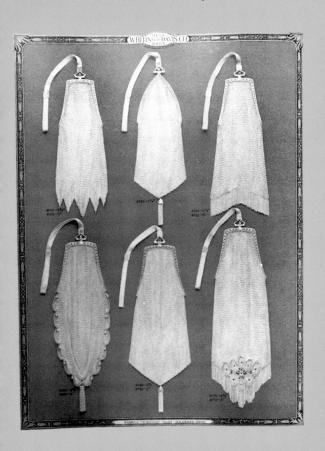

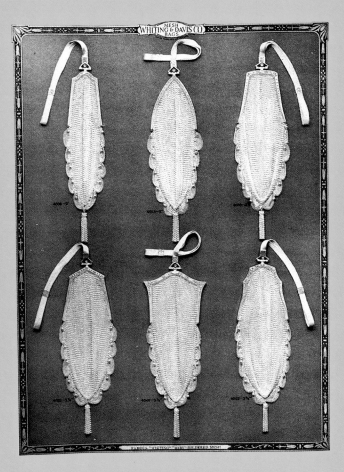

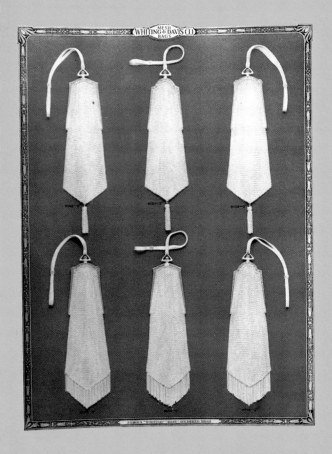

One innovative design incorporated a bell shaped cap that could be slid open on a fine foxtail chain. 3x10. *From the Collection of Joyce Morgan, Photograph by Harry Barth*

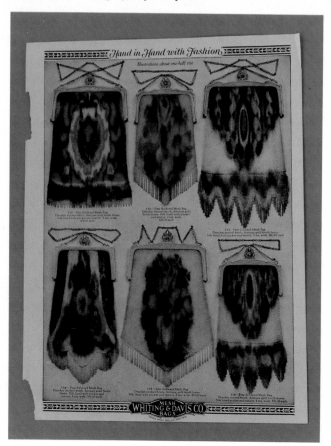

The unmistakable impressionistic quality of the Dresden with a ball and socket closure. A unique interior reveals a watercolored silk lining with sewn pocket. 4x5. *From the Collection of Paula Higgins*

Fine soldered mesh bags in the Dresden style, each silk lined with a pocket and mirror. Wholesale prices ranged from $28.50 to $42.00.

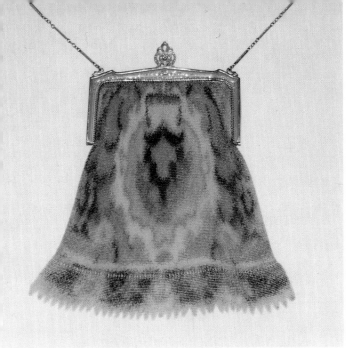

This Dresden sold wholesale for $39.00. 5 1/2x8. *From the Collection of Leslie Holms*

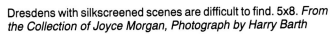

Dresdens with silkscreened scenes are difficult to find. 5x8. *From the Collection of Joyce Morgan, Photograph by Harry Barth*

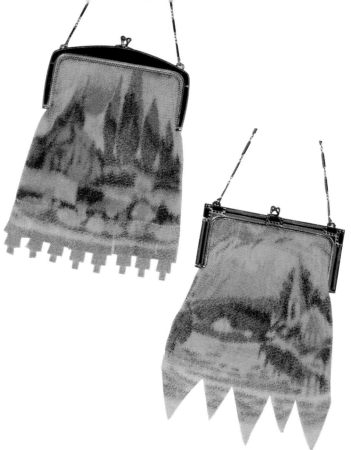

A Dresden with cutout fringe and another with an enameled frame and marcasites. 5 1/2x8. *From the Collection of Leslie Holms*

6x9 1/2. *From the Collection of Leslie Holms*

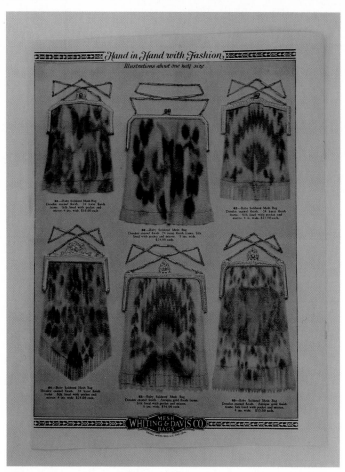

These baby soldered Whiting and Davis Dresden style mesh bags sold wholesale in prices ranging from $18.00 to $36.00 and included silk linings, pockets and mirrors.

A decorative chain fringe and rosette cut out design finishes this bag. 3 1/2x6. *From the Collection of Leslie Holms*

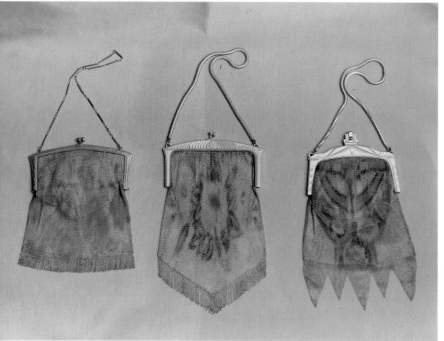

The left and middle examples have Bacchus fringe, all in pretty pastel colors. 5x6 & two are 5x8 1/2. *From the Collection of Paula Higgins*

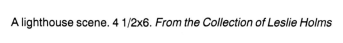

A lighthouse scene. 4 1/2x6. *From the Collection of Leslie Holms*

A striking flame motif Dresden with an ornately embossed frame. 5x6. *From the Collection of Paula Higgins*

A house and landscape scene. 4x5. *From the Collection of Leslie Holms*

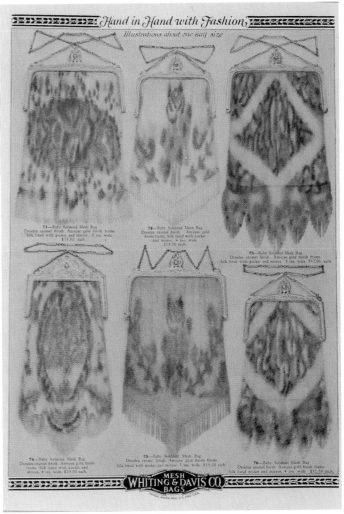

Wholesale prices ranged from $31.50 to $42.00.

A very large flat enameled mesh bag with a bold pattern and cleverly shaped frame. 9 1/2x12. *From the Collection of Joyce Morgan, Photograph by Harry Barth*

This purse advertisement makes no mention of a Whiting and Davis manufacture although they were the only ones who made this type of Dresden bag. *Montgomery Ward, 1932*

A rare combination of enameled armor mesh and fine ring mesh. 4x6 1/2. *From the Collection of Joyce Morgan, Photograph by Harry Barth*

To the left is a narrow bag with Venetian fringe measuring 2 1/2x5 1/2, on the right a black enameled frame with stones and marcasites that measures 5 1/2x8. *From the Collection of Leslie Holms*

Two of these bags have unusual flared skirts. They have gold or silver plated finishes and wholesale prices ranged from $10.50 to $18.00.

Beadlite was a sturdy mesh alternative for the popular beaded bag. 4 1/2x6 3/4. *From the Collection of Paula Higgins*

A rare naturalistic depiction of grape bunches in baby flat mesh. 4x6 1/2. *Author's Collection, Photograph by Dan Civitello*

The *El–Sah* pastel colored fine ring mesh. 4x6 1/2. *From the Collection of Paula Higgins*

The Visitor's Motor Car—
The vagaries of suburban trains and trolley cars need have no terrors for one who would visit the Whiting and Davis plant. As part of the "factory equipment" this car is at your service and will meet you in Boston, Providence, or wherever most convenient, to bring you to Plainville whenever you choose to make an appointment.

The President's Private Office—Mr. Whiting, president and treasurer of Whiting & Davis Company, at his desk. Here the visitor's tour begins and ends—and in between there is the busy maze wherein bars of solid metal are spun into threads of gold and silver and woven into many shapes and patterns of modern mesh bags.

In the assembly room skilled artisans with delicate tools and little jets of gas–flame solder the joints and ball knobs onto the frames.

The Visitor's Dining Room—Yes, this a part of the factory itself! And here Mr. Whiting plays the host at noon. It is a subtle compliment to simple New England cooking that Mr. Whiting seldom dines alone. This little nook is very plain, very quiet, but very convenient in a little town more famous for mesh bags than for restaurants.

5x7. *From the Collection of Joyce Morgan, Photograph by Harry Barth*

Advertisement includes the new "tapestry mesh." *The Ladies Home Journal, October 1924*

Rare enameled flat mesh bag manufactured for The World's Fair. The front reads "Fort Dearborn, Century of Progress, 1833 Chicago 1933." The frame is stamped with The World's Fair insignia. 4x5 1/2. *From the Collection of Joyce Morgan, Photograph by Harry Barth*

This rare bag has a stone set in each enameled diamond shape with an innovative scalloped shaped frame. 5x9 1/2. *From the Collection of Joyce Morgan, Photograph by Harry Barth*

A bold geometric pattern with a unique wide openwork frame that has long jaws to create a wide opening. 3x7. *From the Collection of Joyce Morgan, Photograph by Harry Barth*

Rigid enameled mesh compact/purse with linked tassel. 2x3. *From the Collection of Joyce Morgan, Photograph by Harry Barth*

Whiting and Davis advertisement for flat or armor enameled mesh bags ranging in wholesale price from $4.00 to $18.00.

A lighthouse scene with vandyke fringe. 4x6 3/4. *From the Collection of Paula Higgins*

The fire breathing dragon is a rare Whiting and Davis enameled mesh bag and originally had a pendant drop. 4x6 3/4. *The Curiosity Shop, Photograph by Walter Kitik*

A colorful fiery motif with an enameled frame. 5x6 1/2. *From the Collection of Joyce Morgan, Photograph by Harry Barth*

Baby flat mesh enameled to create a peculiar but beautiful pattern. The frame has a seldom used geometric design. 5x7 1/2. *From the Collection of Joyce Morgan, Photograph by Harry Barth*

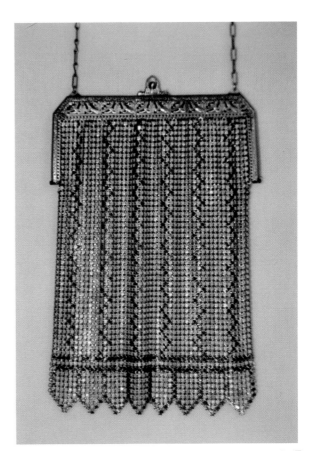

Large bag with pierced frame and Vandyke bottom. 7x10. *From the Collection of Paula Higgins*

Whiting and Davis mesh bags were sometimes compared to beaded bags in advertisements.

Baby flat mesh in unique ivy design. 4x6. *The Curiosity Shop*

Enameled mesh bags with gold or silver plating ranging in wholesale price from $4.50 to $15.00.

Ivorytone flat enameled mesh in pretty golden geometric rug pattern. 4x6. *From the Collection of Paula Higgins*

Ivorytone flat enameled mesh in a refreshing floral design. 4x6.
The Curiosity Shop

Montgomery Ward, 1932

With over 1200 purse frames manufactured by Whiting & Davis, this is a more uncommon one. 5x7. *From the Collection of Joyce Morgan, Photograph by Harry Barth*

4x5 1/2. *From the Collection of Joyce Morgan, Photograph by Harry Barth*

The phenomenal Hollywood Star Series by Whiting and Davis. This rare set of portrait purses from The Heritage Collection was manufactured approximately twenty–five years ago and sold for only $10.00 each. They have extra long carry chains with a rounded spider mesh link. The Charlie Chaplin bag was the only one issued in black and white. There has been conflicting opin-ion as to the reason they were discontinued. Previously, it was assumed that these lovely purses were withdrawn because of lack of demand. More recently, rumors have surfaced indicating that they were purposely recalled and destroyed as a result of lawsuit threats by the star's heirs. 3 1/2x6. *From the Collection of Joyce Morgan, Photograph by Harry Barth*

Renee Adoree.

Marion Davis.

Clark Gable.

Charlie Chaplin.

Mandalian

Sahatiel Garabed Mandalian, born in 1869 in Armenia, Turkey, immigrated to the United States in 1889 and settled in North Attleboro, Massachusetts. Artistically gifted, he attended the Rhode Island School of Design and made himself familiar with all the new customs. When he met the young woman Lillian Green Fuller from Wilton, Maine, he was quite taken by this person with a background so different from his own, and she was similarly captivated by his impeccable reputation, sterling character and unquestionable integrity. In 1903, they were married. In the early years of his business career, Mandalian formed the partnership company of Casper and Mandalian to manufacture jewelry and novelties.

In 1906, Eugene A. Hawkins entered the partnership replacing Mr. Casper and the firm became known as Mandalian & Hawkins. During this time, the company began extensive production of mesh purses. The North Attleboro Board of Trade published this statement in 1913:

> The firm of Mandalian & Hawkins is well known as one of the largest manufacturers of mesh bags in the trade. Organized some six years ago, the concern has been extraordinarily successful. They make one of the most complete lines of unbreakable mesh bags in the country, from the finest link to the coarsest link. Besides making ring mesh, they also are the originators and sole producers of the well–known, machine–made fish scale mesh. Their designs are specially created and thoroughly artistic. The company occupies the entire first floor of the Manufacturer's Building, and employs a large number of hands.

Mesh bags were manufactured under the name Mandalian & Hawkins until 1915 when Mandalian purchased Hawkin's interest and changed the name to The Mandalian Manufacturing Company. This new name was stamped on the inside of the

A postcard depicting the Manufacturer's Building where The Mandalian Company was located. *Courtesy of Ann J. Chapdelaine*

metal frames. Mandalian foresaw the potential in the mesh industry and began a full-fledged effort to create highly desirable and aesthetic purses. The first fish scale mesh machine was invented and perfected under his supervision. This was a unique process, secretly created to produce an unusual glow on furnace-fired enameled links. As part of the advertising campaign, the company promoted "pearlized mesh." This trademarked name was imprinted on celluloid and paper tags as well as on the presentation boxes for the purses. Some of these mesh purses can still be found today in their original boxes. Purses found with the original tags or boxes are a little more valuable now.

The Mandalian purses differ from those made by their primary competitor Whiting & Davis in several ways. Mandalian designs were chiefly florals influenced by the Victorian era and Near Eastern carpet patterns that reminded Mr. Mandalian of his native Turkey. Other designs were naturalistic depictions of birds and butterflies. Jeweled and enameled frames were combined with enameled armor mesh links to create an overall superior purse design. Ornate frames with stamped openwork and elaborate etching were also used. Mandalian pioneered the occasional use of fairly heavy teardrop-shaped metal drops instead of fringe to create a dramatic effect. Bags can be found with the original silk lining and tiny pockets sewn into them. Sometimes, a beveled glass mirror still can be found attached to the lining. High quality was Mandalian's goal. In contrast, the Whiting & Davis manufacturing philosophy was concentrated on a somewhat more mass-produced, geometric and Art Deco design with the emphasis on creating an affordable product made with less handwork.

The Mandalian Company presented a specialty feature called Baby Mesh which was a special type of armor link. The Baby Mesh links were about half the size of the average armor link and more difficult to enamel taking longer to produce and yielding a more desirable product. Smaller links allowed for a more supple flow to the material. Baby Mesh purses were usually made into larger, superior and more expensive purses. Special care was given to the frames that were to be wired to these purses since, often, they were pre-stamped and enameled in many colors.

The Mandalian Manufacturing Company continued with the production of enameled mesh purses until 1944 when the business was sold to Charles A. Whiting and the Whiting & Davis Company. According to the *Evening Chronicle* in North Attleboro, Mr. Mandalian died on June 6, 1949 at the age of 80.

Factory Established 1898 A. D.

Mandalian Manufacturing Co.
SOLE MANUFACTURERS OF
LUSTRO PEARL
Trade Mark
Enameled Mesh Bags

NORTH ATTLEBORO, MASS.

A rarely found Mandalian advertisement. This one promotes the famous lustro-pearl process. *Courtesy of Ann J. Chapdelaine*

Baby mesh with delicate Victorian floral motif and looped chain fringe that is more common on beaded bags. Lovely floral embossed frame compliments the bag. 3 1/4x9. *From the Collection of Joyce Morgan, Photograph by Harry Barth*

A silver scrolled inverted "V" shaped frame with vandyke fringe is the perfect compliment to this lovely enameled mesh double peacock purse. 3 1/2x8. *From the Collection of Paula Higgins*

A Victorian style floral with a dramatic multi–pointed finish. 3 3/4x7. *From the Collection of Joyce Morgan, Photograph by Harry Barth*

Near Eastern carpet motif bags reminded Sahatiel Mandalian of his homeland. This one has baby sized mesh with a decorative enameled and jeweled frame. 5x9. *From the Collection of Joyce Morgan, Photograph by Harry Barth*

Baby mesh floral with two silver birds guarding either side of the ball and socket closure. 4 1/4x9. *From the Collection of Joyce Morgan, Photograph by Harry Barth*

Baby mesh in a floral rug motif pattern. 5x8 1/2. *From the Collection of Joyce Morgan, Photograph by Harry Barth*

Bird themes are difficult to find, especially non–peacock. This motif was also enameled in red, black, and white. 5x8 1/2. *Author's Collection, Photograph by Walter Kitik*

Three advertised Mandalians, although the catalog makes no mention of their manufacturer. Notice the bottom purse is the same as the previously pictured design. *Montgomery Ward, 1932*

Bird of paradise peacocks with sweeping tails, pictured with the box they were purchased in. 4 1/2x8. *Author's Collection, Photograph by Walter Kitik*

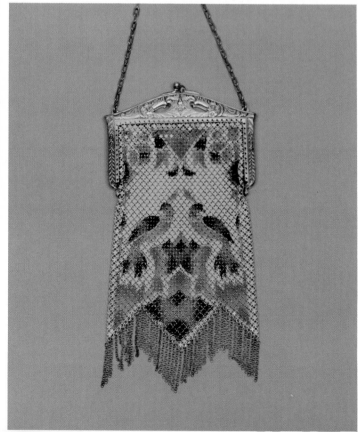

A stylized version of enameled peacocks. The openwork in the frame resembles outlines of two birds. 3 3/4x7. *From the Collection of Joyce Morgan, Photograph by Harry Barth*

100

This exquisite enameled Mandalian with a vase and floral bouquet is a favorite among collectors. 3 1/2x7. *From the Collection of Joyce Morgan, Photograph by Harry Barth*

An elaborate enameled frame was specially manufactured to go perfectly with this bag. 4 1/2x8. *From the Collection of Joyce Morgan, Photograph by Harry Barth*

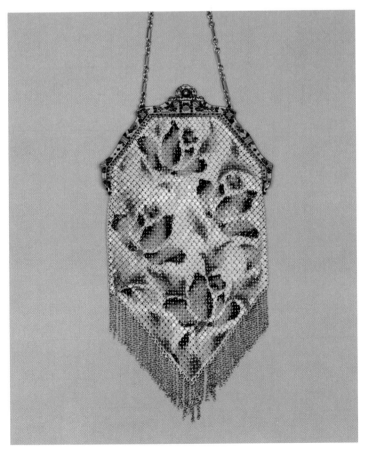

Lovely shaded roses with a striking enameled frame. 5x8. *From the Collection of Joyce Morgan, Photograph by Harry Barth*

Delicately designed triple colored enameled mesh Mandalian with "V" shaped chain fringe. Silvered metal birds adorned the ball and socket closure on the floral enameled frame. 3 1/2x8 1/2. *From the Collection of Paula Higgins*

Exquisite enameled single rose motif with enameled frame. Dramatic multi–pointed mesh finish with calculated sporadically placed chain fringe. 4 1/2x9. *From the Collection of Joyce Morgan, Photograph by Harry Barth*

Rich enameling with teardrop metal finishing and a highly decorative arched floral frame. 4 1/2x8. *From the Collection of Joyce Morgan, Photograph by Harry Barth*

High quality baby mesh with the gleam of the renowned Lustro Pearl finish. Fancy shaped enameled frame, thick chain fringe. 4 1/2x9. *From the Collection of Joyce Morgan, Photograph by Harry Barth*

Tri–colored geometric/floral with black tipped metal teardrops. 4x7. *The Curiosity Shop, Photograph by Walter Kitik*

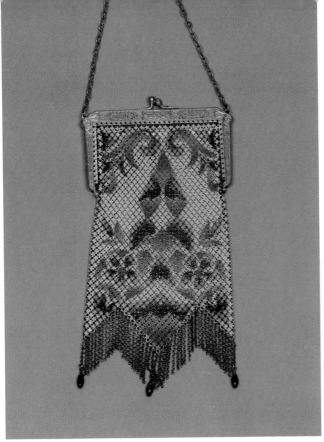

A teardrop and chain fringe combination is a refreshingly different combination. 3 1/2x7. *From the Collection of Joyce Morgan, Photograph by Harry Barth*

A large sized bag in baby mesh with lustro-pearl finish. These bags were sold in fine jewelry stores in boxes and with procedure tags shown here. Notice the unusual looped fringe technique. 4 1/2x9 1/2. *From the Collection of Paula Higgins*

An unusual geometric pattern with the simplest of frames. A metal teardrop finish is desirable. 4x7. *The Curiosity Shop, Photograph by Walter Kitik*

The same floral pattern in a dissimilar color scheme creates a completely new look. Notice the detail in the expensive enameled frame. 4 1/2x9 1/2. *From the Collection of Joyce Morgan, Photograph by Harry Barth*

Two variations of the *Martha Washington,* designed to emulate the brown satin ribbon worked embroidered reticule the famous first lady made and held during George Washington's first inauguration in 1789. *The Curiosity Shop, Photograph by Walter Kitik*

4 1/4x8. *From the Collection of Joyce Morgan, Photograph by Harry Barth*

Vandyke fringe. 5x6 1/4. *From the Collection of Paula Higgins*

Gloria Bags have a unique jointed frame referred to as "bracelet style." One shown here still has the original Lustro Pearl tag. 4 1/4x7. *From the Collection of Joyce Morgan, Photograph by Harry Barth*

With identical frames and patterns, this floral takes on an entirely different look with major color variations. 3 1/2x6. *The Curiosity Shop, Photograph by Walter Kitik*

Flower basket and bird motif silvered frame on an enameled cross hatch and paisley motif bag, extra wide fringe. 4 1/4x8. *From the Collection of Joyce Morgan, Photograph by Harry Barth*

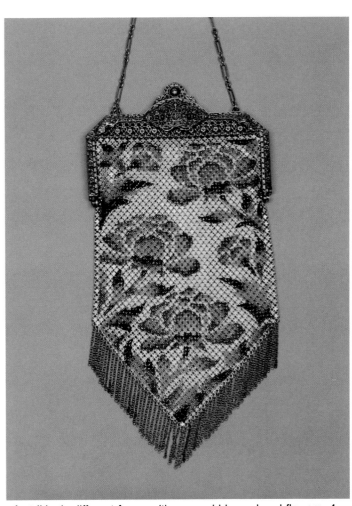

The inverted V-shaped frame on this popular floral designed bag with Vandyke fringe is favored among some collectors. 3 1/2x6. *From the Collection of Joyce Morgan, Photograph by Harry Barth*

A strikingly different frame with unusual blue colored flowers. 4 3/4x9. *From the Collection of Joyce Morgan, Photograph by Harry Barth*

Steel Beaded Purses

Steel beads were manufactured using a blanking process in round and cut (or faceted) shapes. The beads were colored by an electrolytic chemical process producing an extraordinary array of hues. These special beads give the purse a unique sparkle.

Steel beaded purses were made in The United States, Austria, Germany, and France. Those made in America and France are more prevalent. French purses are generally more colorful with a sophisticated design, found often with a label sewn into the silk or satin lining that states: "Made in France," or "Handmade in France." American purses are rarely found signed, although some German and Austrian examples have been found with identifying labels sewn into their linings.

Steel beaded purses are easily distinguished by their heaviness. They are most often confused with the equally weighty, nonferrous beaded purses made of other metals. Quick and easy identification can be obtained with a magnet. Non-steel beads fail to attract when tested.

Made in a large variety of shapes and sizes, categories include: chatelaine, finger ring purses, Tam-O-Shanters, coin purses and misers. Designs are drawstring, pie-shaped, square or envelope style with a flap over top. Similar to their glass beaded counterparts, patterns include scenes, flowers, and geometric shapes. Some frames are quite elaborate with raised silver cherubs, flowers or gargoyles. Many contain a plunger top (a push button soldered to the crest of the frame, designed to be depressed for access to the inside of the purse). Most of these purses have fringe attached to the bottom. The most elaborate fringe consists of decorative lattice work, or the jagged-looking fishnet design. Twisted loops or straight fringe tipped in a loop were popular styles that were also used.

French metallic cut steel beaded bag, elaborately embossed brass frame with jewel accented flowers and lion's head medallion center. Late nineteenth century. 8x14. *From the Collection of Madeline Hofer, Photograph by David Fowler*

Jeweled lion's head frame with plunger top shown up close. *From the Collection of Madeline Hofer, Photograph by David Fowler*

Figural cut steel bags in many colors are difficult to find. The bag pictured has a lovely jewel and rose decorated frame. 7x9 1/2. *From the Collection of Joyce Morgan, Photograph by Harry Barth*

Traditional French cut steel in gold, black and silver. Notice the graceful scroll and leaf design. Embossed frame, ball twist clasp. Double carry chains help support the heavy weight of the steel beads, early twentieth century. 6 1/2x9 1/2. *From the Collection of Paula Higgins*

"Made in France" is sewn on the silk lining of this pretty rose motif cut steel bag, ca. 1900. 4x7. *From the Collection of Madeline Hofer, Photograph by David Fowler*

7x10. *The Curiosity Shop, Photograph by Walter Kitik*

A Middle Eastern motif frame blends nicely with a vibrant colored Persian carpet design on this French purse. 10x15. *From the Collection of Leslie Holms*

Metal beads in a colorful carpet motif pattern. 7x11. *From the Collection of Joyce Morgan, Photograph by Harry Barth*

Grey silk knitted reticule with fine cut steel depiction of a Griffin, European origin. 6x11. *From the Collection of Paula Higgins*

Fine cut steel beaded floral in reticule form with exquisite detailing at the top and on carry straps. Tightly twisted loop fringe. Made in France. 6 3/4x10 3/4. *From the Collection of Paula Higgins*

The reverse side shows a Phoenix bird. Notice the extra care given to the construction of the fringe. *From the Collection of Paula Higgins*

Cut steel bags with sailboats in a water scene are hard to find. This one is brilliantly colored with an extra wide frame and a plunger top. Silk lining, made in France. 6x10. *From the Collection of Paula Higgins*

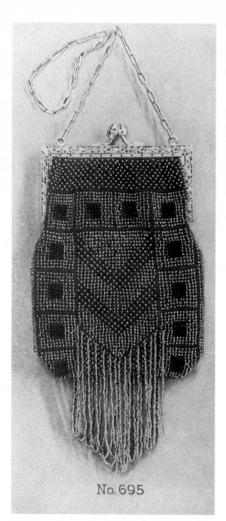

No. 695

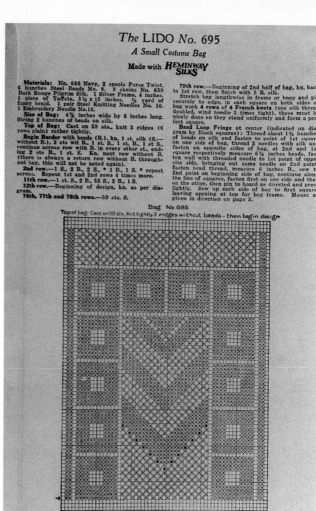

The LIDO No. 695
A Small Costume Bag
Made with HEMINWAY SILKS

Materials: No. 666 Navy, 2 spools Purse Twist. 6 bunches Steel Beads No. 8. 3 skeins No. 659 Dark Rouge Pilgrim Silk. 1 Silver Frame, 4 inches. 1 piece of Taffeta, 5½ x 13 inches. ½ yard of fancy braid. 1 pair Steel Knitting Needles No. 16. 1 Embroidery Needle No.18.

Size of Bag: 4⅞ inches wide by 6 inches long. String 2 bunches of beads on silk.

Top of Bag: Cast on 59 sts., knit 3 ridges (6 rows plain) rather tightly.

Begin Border with beads (B.), kn. 1 st. silk (S.— without B.), 2 sts wit B. 1 st. S. 1 st B., 1 st S., continue across row with B. in every other st., ending 2 sts B., 1 st. S. Kn. next row without B. (there is always a return row without B., throughout bag, this will not be noted again).

2nd row.—1 S., 2 B., 2 S. * 1 B, 1 S. * repeat across. Repeat 1st and 2nd rows 4 times more.

11th row.—1 st. S., 2 B. 53 S. 2 B., 1 S.

12th row.—Beginning of design, kn. as per diagram.

76th, 77th and 78th rows.—59 sts. S.

79th row.—Beginning of 2nd half of bag, kn. back to 1st row, then finish with 3 R. silk.

Stretch bag lengthwise in frame or hoop and pin securely to edge, in each square on both sides of bag work 4 rows of 4 French knots (use silk thread doubled, wind needle 3 times tight), these must be nicely done so they stand uniformly and form a perfect square.

Bead Loop Fringe at center (indicated on diagram by Black squares): Thread about 1½ bunches of beads on silk and fasten to point of 1st square on one side of bag, thread 2 needles with silk and fasten on opposite sides of bag, at 2nd and 1st square respectively measure 6½ inches beads, fasten well with threaded needle to 1st point of opposite side, bringing out same needle on 2nd point, fasten bead thread, measure 6 inches B., sew to 2nd point on beginning side of bag, continue along the line of squares, fasten first on one side and then on the other, then pin to board as directed and press lightly. Sew up each side of bag to first square, leaving opening at top for bag frame. Mount as given in direction on page 3.

Bag No. 695

Top of bag - Cast on 59 sts. Knit tightly 3 ridges without beads - then begin design.

knit 3 ridges plain - then begin design at dart for 2nd half of bag - Length 6 inches. Width 4⅞ inches.

Design in steel beads. Black squares ■ indicate where to attach fringe for each side of bag.

Pattern and instructions to make the American steel bag called *The Lido* The Book of Bags, ca 1920

A fleur–de–lis pattern with cut steel. Unusual gilt embossed frame with applied bow, garland and acorn twist clasp, Art Nouveau period. 6x9. *From the Collection of Madeline Hofer, Photograph by David Fowler*

A moonlit scene of Chinese junks at sea, silver plating over embossed and openworked white metal frame with jewels and enamel. Plunger top, silk lining, early twentieth century. 6x10. *From the Collection of Madeline Hofer, Photograph by David Fowler*

Rug motif reticule in pretty pastel colors with lattice style fringe, French. 6 1/2x9 1/2. *From the Collection of Leslie Holms*

No.690

"Smart for afternoon and of ample size for evening, vanity and lorgnette bag" is the description given for *The Naida* knitted bag suggested to be made with navy silk and steel beads. *The Book of Bags, ca. 1920*

French reticule with unusual fringe. 8 1/2x12 1/2. *From the Collection of Leslie Holms*

No. 1573—BEADED ENVELOPE BAG—This dainty little bag when made, measures 6¼x4½ inches. The materials consist of stamped black satin; one metal rod, crinoline, thread, beading needles and sufficient beads. Price with No. 4 metal beads, $3.00. Made to order, $10.00. With best quality cut crystal luster beads, $1.95. Made to order, $9.00. Stamped pattern alone, 50 cents.

This beaded envelope bag with steel beads cost $10.00. *Bead Craft, The Art Beautiful, 1934*

No. 683

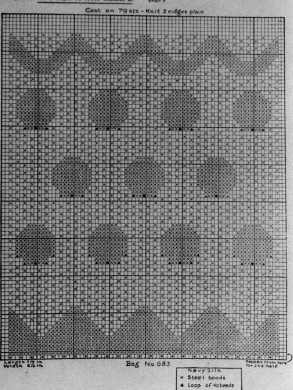

The GALLIENE No. 683
Striking Bag in Blue and Steel
Made with HEMINWAY SILKS

Materials: No. 666 Navy Blue, 2 spools Purse Twist. 10 bunches Steel Beads No. 8. 1 Silver Frame 6 inches. 1 piece of Taffeta 8 x 15 inches. ½ yard Silver Braid. 1 pair Steel Knitting Needles No. 16.

Size of Bag: Width, 7 inches; length flat, 14 inches; length 7 inches made up. (S.—Silk without beads. Beads—B.) Thread 2 bunches of B. or silk.

Top of Bag: Cast on 79 sts. (There is always a return row plain kn. throughout bag, this is not noted again.) Kn. 2 ridges (4 rows) without B.

3rd ridge (R.)—Kn. 2 sts. S., 1 st. with B., * 4 sts. S., 1 st. B., 3 sts. S., 1 st. B., 3 sts. S., 1 st. B., 3 sts. S., 3 sts. S. * repeat from * to * 3 times, end 1 st. B., 2 sts. S. Repeat from 3rd R. according to diagram to the 28th. The Black squares and triangles represent loops which are kn. in across row as noted in diagram. The circles at bottom on 59th R. are for loops of fringe, also continue from 89th R. back to 1st R. for opposite side of bag. Fold bag and sew up sides, leaving 2 inches opening at top for bag frame. Mount bag as given in directions on page 2

Cast on 79 sts. - Knit 2 ridges plain

Length 7½ in
Width 6½ in.   Bag No G683   Repeat from here for 2nd half

Navy Silk
× Steel beads
▲ Loop of 40 beads
■ Loop of 45 beads
● Loop of 60 beads

Pattern and directions for making The Galliene, an Amerian cut steel wtih filigree frame. *The Book of Bags, ca. 1920*

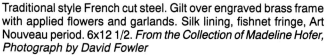

Traditional style French cut steel. Gilt over engraved brass frame with applied flowers and garlands. Silk lining, fishnet fringe, Art Nouveau period. 6x12 1/2. *From the Collection of Madeline Hofer, Photograph by David Fowler*

Few fine French cut steel bags with figures in multiple colors can be found in as good condition as this one. Elaborate lattice fringe, plunger top. 8x12. *From the Collection of Joyce Morgan, Photograph by Harry Barth*

Textiles

From the eleventh to the fourteenth centuries, needlework in Europe was hand constructed primarily in monasteries and convents. Each embroiderer was an expert or a student on the way to becoming one. Most of the items that children made in the convents were used in the church or by the clergy. Sometimes, these children returned to the world outside the convent and used their training and talent to support themselves by selling their handiwork.

During the nineteenth century in the United States, learning and practicing various forms of needlework became popularly fashionable for young women. At this time, homemakers did not do paid work unless poverty forced them to the mills, so many ladies--it seems any who could hold a needle--were embroidering something in the Victorian era! Beautiful satin-stitched, petitpoint, and needlework purses were made as a hobby, and later were used for personal enjoyment.

Purse embroideries are divided into two classes: flat (art) embroidery and decorative (raised novelty) embroidery. Flat embroidery includes all ornamental needlework of crewel, tapestry, wool, silk, linen, cotton, metallic or gold threads applied directly to the fabric of the background of the purse. Embroideries wrought of chenille have been termed raised novelty embroidery.

The process of covering open space in a canvas between the warp and weft threads, using a threaded needle to place stitches across from one opening to the next in a diagonal direction, is called "needlepoint." The term used to identify extremely fine work of this type in stitches half the size of the needlepoint stitch is "petitpoint." The term for larger stitches, nearing twice the area of the needlepoint stitch, is "gross point."

Chinese embroidery made with silk was quite popular in the United States from the turn of the century to the 1920s. Purses made with Chinese embroidery were colorful and often had solid jade or glass bracelet rings instead of carrying chains. Ladies' magazines advertised these imported purses.

The tapestry stitch, used in embroidery and in Berlin work, is raised from the canvas by being worked over two horizontal threads. Tapestry purses were woven by hand or by machines.

The satin stitch, generally used in old French embroidery on silk and flannel, is worked by passing a thread from one outline of the design to the other, back and forth, leaving an equal amount of material on both sides of the work. These patterns should be run through with filling stitches to leave the work, when finished, slightly raised and with a rounded effect.

It is nice to consider embroidered purses as family heirlooms passing from one generation to the next, linking people who may not have met.

Silk embroidered French figural with detailed filigree fittings for crown set faux emeralds. 6x6 1/2. *From the Collection of Joyce Morgan, Photograph by Harry Barth*

"Embroidery Lessons

WITH COLORED STUDIES" FOR 1911

☞ OUR LATEST BOOK ON EMBROIDERY ☜

This is an entirely new and fresh number of our annual publication Each year's publication is better than the last. THIS BEST OF ALL. Contains the designs that will be popular and stylish ones the coming season. Don't spend your time on designs that will be "out of date" when finished.

Price 16c. a Copy.

(AFTER SEEING THE BOOK, YOU WOULD NOT PART WITH YOUR COPY FOR THREE TIMES THE PRICE.)

This Instructive New Number of our "Embroidery Lessons with Colored Studies" will keep you "abreast of the times" in working Centerpieces, Doilies, Table Covers, Sofa Cushions, etc.

Special Features shown by its 150 pages and hundreds of illustrations are :

Diagrams for Beginners, showing Color Distribution and Stitch Slant for many different flowers — nothing could make the work more simple.

☞ Colored Plates showing how to embroider popular flowers, Centerpieces, Doilies, Sofa Cushions, etc.

☞ Round and Oval Centers.

☞ Coronation Braid Designs.

☞ Eyelet and Wallachian Designs.

☞ Handsome Table and Bureau Scarfs.

☞ Pin Cushions and Jabots.

☞ Shirt Waists and Underwear.

☞ Sofa Cushions and Dainty Novelties.

This is not merely an instruction book, but our COMPLETE LINEN CATALOGUE, showing a splendid line of stamped goods that our Linen Department carries in stock. Send 16 cents (2c. stamps accepted) and ask for our BOOK FOR 1911. Not sent for Holders or Tags.

THE BRAINERD & ARMSTRONG COMPANY,
100 UNION ST., NEW LONDON, CONN.

Embroidery Lessons with Colored Studies

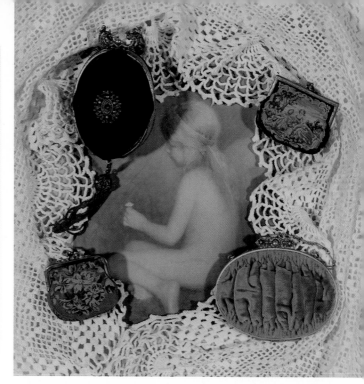

Clockwise: petitpoint figural coin purse with ball and twist closure, tan velvet oval silk lined purse with green enamel flowers on either side of ball and socket closure, floral petitpoint coin purse, and an unusual jewel encrusted oval dance bag with gilt brass findings. *The Curiosity Shop*

Fine classical Austrian petitpoint on fine gauze with different scenes on both sides. Beige silk lining with card case in pocket, early twentieth century. 7x7 1/4. *From the Collection of Paula Higgins*

114

An original petitpoint scenic canvas pattern, handstamped in color, complete with different scenes for each side of the bag and a carry strap outline. A rare find in its original state. European origin. *The Curiosity Shop, Photograph by Dan Civitello*

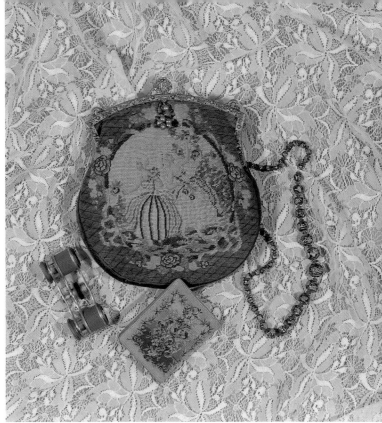

Rose picking in a garden is displayed with this petitpoint featuring a faux jewel encrusted frame pictured with a floral wallet. Unusual pendant ornamentation. 8x10. *The Curiosity Shop, Photograph by Dan Civitello*

Exquisite silk velvet corduroy bag with applied scenic and flower/leaf ornamentation fashioned of hand colored, wire twisted fibers. Tassel drops consist of metal ring–encased fiber and cording, constructed of braided metallic wrapped fabric. Gilded frame embellished with Empire figure heads and double hand–wrought chain handle. "Norman 1" is impressed into the frame. 7x10. *From the Collection of Madeline Hofer, Photograph by David Fowler*

Tapestry with elaborate wide sterling frame transformed into shapes of birds, roses, flowers, ribbons, and swans. 8x10. *The Curiosity Shop, Photograph by Walter Kitik*

Patterns and instructions for four embroidered and woven tapestry bags. *The Book of Bags, ca. 1920*

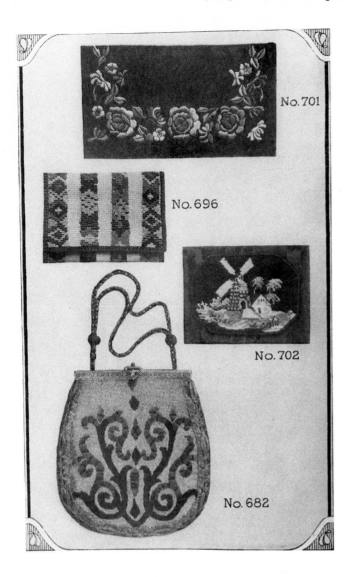

No. 701

No. 696

No. 702

No. 682

The SYRIENNE No. 682
Unusual Bag in Embroidered Tapestry—It Lends Individuality and Distinction to the Smart Costume

Made with **HEMINWAY SILKS**

Materials: Nos. 2244 or 2279 Dull Bronze, 20 skeins; Nos. 149, 464, 462 Dull Blue Violet, 4 skeins each; No. 494 Grape, 3 skeins; Nos. 492, 2286 Grape, 1 skein each; No. 944 Green Blue, 1 skein; No. 1 Black, 1 skein Texto Rope (Artificial Silk). ¾ yd. Antique Gold Galloon. 10 inch width of Canvas. 1 French Gilt Collapsible 6-inch Bag Frame.

Size of Bag: Length finished, 8¾ inches. Widest point at bottom, 8½ inches. Width at top, 6¼ inches.

Perforated Design and exact size of bag sent upon receipt of 35c. Design worked out on both sides of bag. Stamp pattern on canvas and place in frame, each small section of design is worked (top and down) in straight or slanting satin stitch, using more of darker tones. On perforated design the colors are marked where used. Tapestry background No. 2244 is then worked in, edges of design must be

kept even when working in background. Long and short stitches extending across the bag (its width), after this is completed 1 st. of No. 494 across the design outlines the sections. The work is very easy to accomplish and one feels proud to be the possessor of a bag which speaks richly in style and coloring of the present day tapestry vogue. Press carefully on soft blankets, cut canvas ½ inch beyond line of embroidery, sew carefully the 2 sides together in a flat seam. Mount bag as given on page 3. Apply the galloon over the seam and around entire bag.

The cord handle is braided, using 1 skein each of Nos. 2244, 2286, 944 and 464, double the length and braid the 4 colors together, pull through rings of bag frame and double, joining at one side under the braided rings made of No. 149 as follows: Make a round clasp braided with 4 threads (doubled), wind round the 2 cords an inch from ends and fasten neatly.

The VIKING No. 696
See page 21 for description

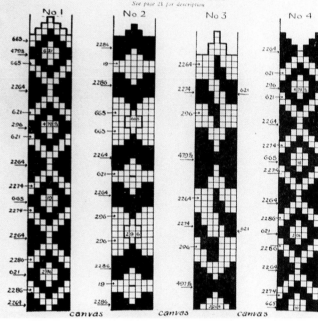

The HAGUE No. 702
See page 25 for description, and photographic illustration on page 12

×	- 341
⊞	- 585
◨	- 345
▷	- 343
⊙	- 34
□	- 2010
●	- 824
◼	- 582
▪	- 35
-	- 2119
▯	- 14
◺	- 1621
⫶	- 63
⯀	- 104

No 702 Bag in Petit-Point Embroidery.

[11]

The VIKING No. 696
See diagram on page 13
An Envelope Bag in Woven Tapestry—One of the Latest French Novelties

Made with **HEMINWAY SILKS**

Materials: No. 1 Black, 12 skeins; Nos. 479½ American Beauty, 665 Navy, 2264 Jade, 2 skeins each; Nos. 19 Gold, 296 Medium Blue, 621 Maize, 2274 Tancerne, 2286 Fuchsia, 1 skein each Texto Rope (Artificial Silk). 1 piece Beige Tricot Canvas 11 x 18 inches (extra amount for frame), ½ yard Satin for lining. ½ yard Flannel, ½ yard Buckram. 1 Chenille Needle (dull point). Nos. 18 or 20.

Note: To keep size of bag to measurements it may be necessary to add extra mesh to plain rows of canvas between the weaving bands as mesh of canvas often varies in size.

Size of Bag: Finished folded about 5¾ x 7½ inches. Length flat 16 inches.

Commence by pulling lengthwise threads of canvas (7 square meshes—1 inch), leave 1 inch (7 meshes) width of canvas, draw lengthwise another inch band, repeat twice more, there are 3 bands of canvas and 4 bands of weaving. Sample of weaving shows how work is carried on, diagram places colorings where indicated by darts.

Border is done first around entire bag, working over 4 mesh in satin stitch, keeping 1 st. of silk between each thread of canvas, this keeps a clean even line on both sides of bag, which is the main thing of beauty throughout work, the uniformity of st.

To do the weaving thread needle with 1 strand of Texto Rope, needle up at beginning corner, down over 4 threads or mesh of canvas equal to 1 check on diagram, under 4 threads, up over 4 threads, this covers 3 mesh. Return row of weaving, needle back under last 4 threads, up over 4 threads, down under the next 4 threads, repeat weaving 3 times more, this completes 3 meshes of No. 1. Continue in this manner to complete Green sections, then work upward, the empty meshes of design are also woven in; the same as the dark meshes. The 3 spaces between weaving is plain canvas. This is a very easy and simple method of developing a most unusual bag both in coloring and stitch. Nos. 1 and 4 columns of weaving are the same design. Press well on soft wool padding with a medium iron. Fold back canvas to edge of Black border. Cut stiff buckram the exact size of embroidered canvas, then cut 2 pieces thin flannel lining, each ½-inch wider, stretch flannel over both sides of buck-

Showing method of working stitches in completing Swedish Embroidery on Bag No. 696
Color Plan Page 13

ram lining, turn in edges and baste around. Cut a piece of satin lining of desired shade 11 inches long x 6½ inches deep, stitch in casing at top with ½ inch heading, through casing run elastic, shirring satin to 7 inches in length. Sew pocket to satin 6 inches from one end of bag, pacing on bottom. Depth of pocket 4¾ inches exact. For 2 pockets featherstitch down depth. Lay satin on both sides over flannel and sl. st. around. Sew embroidery on top side neatly and fold. Turn back other end 4¾ inches to form bag pocket and sl. st. or buttonhole the 2 sides together; buttonholing may be continued around lap of bag if desired.

[21]

SILK flower-bordered envelope bag embroidered in veritable Chinese colors. The complementary tones of yellowed browns of the Wild Chrysanthemum, old soft pinks of the Cherry, combined with grayish-green foliage, form just the background desired for the shades of dull rose and gobelin blues used in the three outstanding flowers. The various color reflections make it very useful to carry with many gowns. It may also be simplified to browns or greens; poudre blues or tangerines to conform in color with the modish tailleur. This drawing is exact size of design on bag.

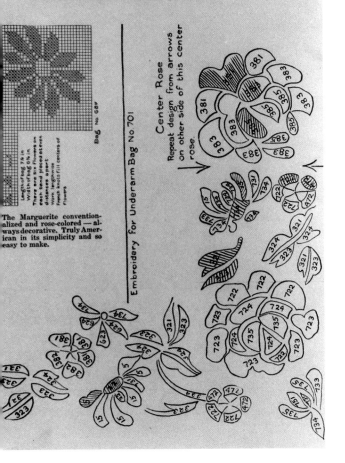

The Marguerite conventionalized and rose-colored — always decorative. Truly American in its simplicity and so easy to make.

A select group of quality petitpoints including a figural calling card holder and a wallet along with two coin purses. None larger than 3x4, most with sixty stitches to the square inch. *The Curiosity Shop, Photograph by Walter Kitik*

Woven floral tapestry with cabochon decoration on frame. 7x10. *The Curiosity Shop, Photograph by Walter Kitik*

Stylish silk embroidered figural with arched jeweled frame. 4 1/2x5 1/2. *From the Collection of Joyce Morgan, Photograph by Harry Barth*

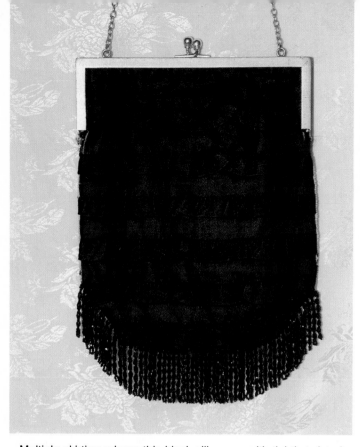

Multiple skirting adorns this black silk purse with tightly twisted glass beaded fringe. 7x9. *From the Collection of Paula Higgins*

Floral petitpoint. 5x6. *The Curiosity Shop, Photograph by Walter Kitik*

Turn of the century silk chenille embroidered purse on gold metallic gauze. Gold frame set with multicolor cabochon jewels. Pretty metal flower baskets connect the frame to the carry chain. 4x6. *From the Collection of Paula Higgins, Photograph by Walter Kitik*

Austrian petitpoint floral with black jewels on overclasp and silk lined interior. Pictured with a petitpoint calling card case. 5x6. *The Curiosity Shop, Photograph by Walter Kitik*

Silk stitched romantic figural in an unconventional oval shape. 3x4. *From the Collection of Joyce Morgan, Photograph by Harry Barth*

Highly uncommon French old roses petitpoint hand stitched on silk mesh with approximately forty stitches to the inch. Black ultra–suede body with expensive gilt goat skin piping. This type of petitpoint on silk mesh is no longer made and sells for hundreds of dollars per yard when available. 5x10. *From the Collection of Joyce Morgan, Photograph by Harry Barth*

Chinese embroidered purse made for the export market. Silk stitched in jewel tone colors interspersed with gold metal thread. Jade bracelet ring, ca. 1910. 9x10. *From the Collection of Paula Higgins*

Early twentieth century silk stitched purse featuring a pastoral eighteenth century scene. Marcasite and jeweled plunger closure. Pale green silk lining, beautiful shading techniques. 5 1/2x8 3/4. *From the Collection of Paula Higgins*

A male Golden Pheasant, with vibrant plumage native to the forests of central China, is depicted on this lovely petitpoint bag featuring a jeweled and enameled frame. 6x8. *The Curiosity Shop, Photograph by Walter Kitik*

Chenille stitched three dimensional floral on black velvet with Deco motif enameled striped frame. 4x4. *The Curiosity Shop, Photograph by Walter Kitik*

Floral embroidery on fine netted gauze, metal wreath pendant drop. 5x5. *The Curiosity Shop, Photograph by Walter Kitik*

Floral embroidered dance bag on fine netting encased in an unusual jeweled gilt and filigree brass circle. Details include a jeweled carry chain and an interior that contains two silk pouches and a mirror on a chain. 3 1/2 diameter. *From the Collection of Joyce Morgan, Photograph by Harry Barth*

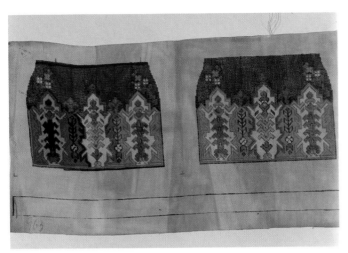

An original petitpoint geometric canvas pattern, handstamped in color, complete with a carry strap outline. Difficult to find in its original state, although this one has been started in the bottom corner of the left side, then abandoned for years. European origin, ca. 1920. *The Curiosity Shop, Photograph by Dan Civitello*

The People's Home Journal, September 1919

Detailed French celluloid leaf motif frame on Elk with piping and celluloid fittings. 6x8. *From the Collection of Cindi St. Clair*

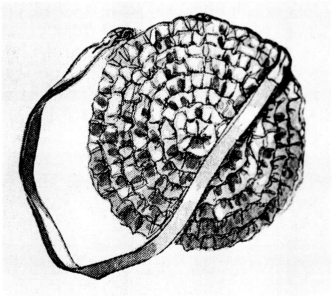

Shirred grosgrain ribbon bag that sold for $8.50. *Fashionable Dress, February 1925*

Hand woven tapestry figural, enameled and faux pearl frame. 6x9. *The Curiosity Shop, Photograph by Walter Kitik*

A lady on a swing is an excellent subject choice for this jeweled tapestry. 7x8. *The Curiosity Shop, Photograph by Walter Kitik*

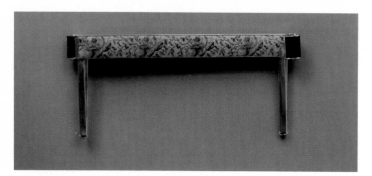

Superbly executed floral petitpoint stitched on an unusual medium; a purse frame fitted with two overclasps in black suede. 7 inches wide. *The Curiosity Shop, Photograph by Walter Kitik*

Swirling silver frame chatelaine purse with silk lining. Extra sturdy carry chain. 6x9. *From the Collection of Paula Higgins*

The People's Home Journal, September 1919

Plastics

"Cellulos nitrate," "pyroxylin," or the more familiar term "celluloid" is the oldest synthetic plastic used in making purses. Discovered in 1856 by English metallurgist Alexander Parkes, it was first called "Parkesine." In the United States, John Wesley Hyatt developed celluloid as a commercial product in 1869. Its strength, luster, and colorability combined with its low cost made it a comparatively inexpensive substitute for ivory and other natural materials. Subsequently, the demand for the material instigated the formation of The Celluloid Manufacturing Company in 1871.

Soon thereafter, celluloid was used to make a wide variety of items including fountain pens, piano keys, tooth brushes, dentures, photographic film, and purses. It was plentiful, easy to work, and could be made into a variety of shapes. Faux jewels could easily be imbedded for decoration into celluloid purses before they hardened completely.

In spite of all these attributes, celluloid is highly flammable and, if ignited, burns furiously. By 1934, celluloid was banned from the market by federal law. However, its discovery as the first synthetic plastic paved the way for more experiments to create better plastics for general use, including purses.

The plastic material known as Bakelite, the trademarked name for synthetic phenolic resin, was discovered and patented in 1909 by Leo Hendrik Baekelund (1863-1944), a Belgian-American chemist, in his private laboratory in Yonkers, New York. It is formed by the combination of phenol and formaldehyde and often is compounded with reinforcing fillers such as wood fibers or cotton lints. Under the influence of heat, the material becomes a hard, insoluble mass which is incombustible. In its pure form, it is colorless or light golden resembling celluloid, but it is much harder and heavier.

The General Bakelite Company was organized in 1910, and in 1922 the company merged with two others to form The Bakelite Corporation. Shortly thereafter, Bakelite flooded the marketplace. It was made into countless industrial and domestic products, including jewelry, poker chips, bottle caps, electric switches, cutlery handles and, of course, ladies' purses. Throughout the Thirties, heavy marbled brown purses with rigid Bakelite handles and shiny yellow carved floral lids were plentiful. The variety of colors soon became astounding and clever accessorizing was affordable. Other firms

Ruby red box shaped Lucite purse by Willardy, ca. 1953–55. 9 1/2x4 1/2x4 1/4. *From the Collection of Kay Miguez, Photograph by Miguez Photography*

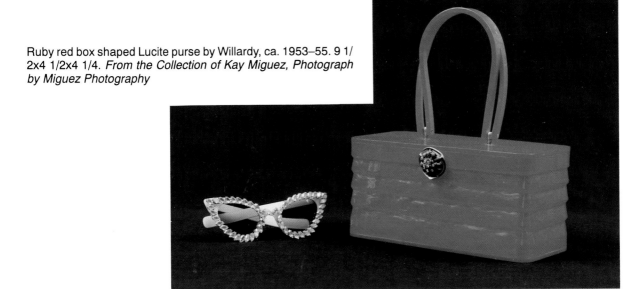

marketed phenolic resin under various trade names.

Lucite and Plexiglas are trade names for polymethyl methacrylate (PMMA), a plastic also known as "acrylic." This plastic has minimal crystallization and high resistance to the ultraviolet radiation of outdoor exposure. With the potential for unlimited coloring possibilities, it is hard and strong although it can be brittle. Lucite has been used for lighting fixtures, outdoor signs, and automobile taillights.

As plastics were entering the fashion circles, Harry Senzer worked for Associated Plastics that made parts for handbags. Purse handles, ornaments, and clasps were sold to different handbag manufacturers all searching for a new look. In the early 1950s, the first simple box-shaped purse was produced entirely of Lucite. It first appeared on the market either colorless or tinted. Soon came acetate plastic which simulated tortoiseshell. Harry Senzer joined a new company called Rialto and contributed significantly to the manufacture of plastic purses that originally sold wholesale for nine dollars apiece. The Rialto designers experimented and added a wide variety of purse shapes and colors to their lines. It became quite stylish to own a Lucite handbag in the 1950s.

Celluloid impressed cherub with leather carry strap. 3 1/4" diameter. *From the Collection of Joyce Morgan, Photograph by Harry Barth*

Two elephant motif celluloid purse frames with sew holes. *The Curiosity Shop, Photograph by Walter Kitik*

Celluloid cherub motif purse in diamond shape with jeweled plunger top and silk tassel. 5x7 *The Curiosity Shop, Photograph by Dan Civitello*

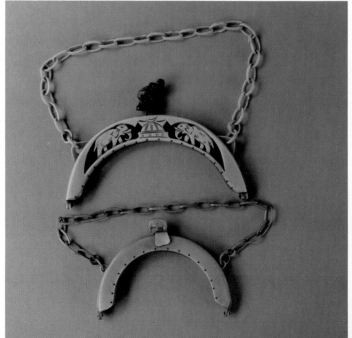

Pretty red impressed celluloid purse contains a mirror inside. 3" diameter. *From the Collection of Joyce Morgan, Photograph by Harry Barth*

An extraordinary wide celluloid flower basket frame in color on a simple brown velvet bag. 5x10. *The Curiosity Shop, Photograph by Walter Kitik*

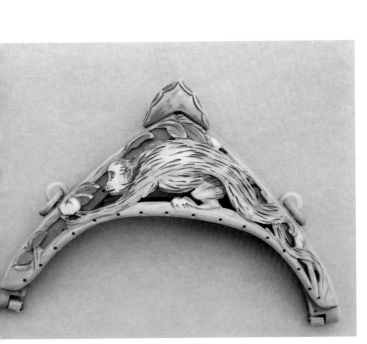

French colored celluloid monkey motif frame with unusual triangular shaped overclasp. *Author's Collection, Photograph by Walter Kitik*

A mirror is inside the lid of this unique egg–shaped Bakelite bag. 2 1/2x4. *From the Collection of Joyce Morgan, Photograph by Harry Barth*

Hinged Bakelite purse in an oriental motif with leather strap. 4" diameter. *The Curiosity Shop, Photograph by Walter Kitik*

Two imitation tortoise colored Bakelite purses. An extensively carved floral design dominates both contrasting yellow lids. The octagon shaped purse is marked "Original Rialto, New York." 6x8 & 4x8. *The Curiosity Shop, Photograph by Walter Kitik*

Vanity Purses

Vanity bags, also known as compact purses, are a novelty whose collectibility is two-fold: they are desirable to purse enthusiasts as well as compact collectors. Vanity bags, usually made in part with mesh and including a compact appurtenance, were manufactured in the 1920s and 1930s. Some were composed entirely of early plastics. A small number were cloth and others can be found in metal or sterling silver, such as the *necessaire* which is a small bolster-shaped combination of compact and purse. Many such purses were intended for late afternoon or evening wear by discriminating, well dressed women. Companies that manufactured vanity purses include Whiting & Davis, Evans, Bliss–Napier, and R & G.

Innovative designs that incorporate the compact into the purse in new ways are a delight to find. Consider the Napier–Bliss Du Barry Bag in which the compact is connected not to the frame, as was most often done, but to the braided mesh carry strap. When not in use, the powder box lay in the hand while the purse was carried. The Du Barry Bag was promoted as "the perfect combination mesh bag and powder box," and advertisements depict a woman holding the bag and, simultaneously, using the powder case with ease. The Du Barry Bag was introduced to the jewelry industry through an announcement in *The Jeweler's Circular* trade publication. After the initial introduction, it was advertised in *Vogue* to reach retail buyers. It had a lovely arched frame, fine mesh body, metal fringed tassel and an artistically carved powder case, available in 14 karat green gold, gold filled, sterling and the company's innovative Nile–Gold. The bag was sold through fine quality jewelry stores.

Many ingenious vanity purses were introduced by The Whiting & Davis Company. The Delysia is arguably the most unique vanity bag that this company made, and it is, without question, highly desirable today. The compact portion of this bag is encased in metal bands in the center, rather than the more customary positioning in the frame at the top. A pocket of mesh is found on the top and on the bottom of the bag where it is adorned with a tassel. Carry strap positioning is at the top center of the bag attached to a metal reinforcement cap that was artfully crafted and etched. Frame bands encompassing the center of the bag have fine detailing. A Delysia featured in *Cosmopolitan* in December of 1924 contained two mirrors, a powder and rouge compact. It was made in gold, silver, sunset mesh, and what was promoted as "colored tapestry mesh," which was a glorified way of advertising enameling. Whiting Davis called The Delysia the "utility mesh bag." This bag was sold at prestigious jewelry stores and could also be found in jewelry departments at fine stores in prices ranging from five to five-hundred dollars.

Whiting & Davis also introduced The Baby Peggy purse that came in gold, silver, or enameled mesh and was meant for "her" daughter. The manufacturer cleverly described it as "grown up in every way but in price." The bottom of the bag is mesh but the top is silk. It could be drawn to a close with a pull cord instead of the mesh capped adult version that had a carry strap. This variation helped to keep the manufacturing cost low while still maintaining the general appearance of The Delysia.

The Piccadilly was a popular vanity purse made in the Twenties. In it, a round compact was incorporated into the frame at the top of the bag. The bodies of these purses are usually made with fine ring or baby soldered mesh, but one of the few exceptions was The New Piccadilly which had a large rose and foliage enameled onto armor mesh links. It contains soft powder and rouge with sifters referred to as "loose–pact" and "rouge–pact."

The El–Sah vanity purse has a rectangular compact as part of the frame. Compact lids were enameled in floral designs, jeweled, or had a black silhouette of a man and woman in a dance pose. When the compact is contained within the frame of the purse in this fashion, access to the compact portion is gained when the thumbpiece is depressed and the lid is lifted up. Inside, the compact top has an oval mirror and a clip to hold a comb. The jewel and enamel crested El–Sah has an additional metal plate that separates the powder from a calling card holder. On the bottom are two pots, holding compressed powder and rouge, with individual, silk-lined puffs. Entrance to the purse portion is attained by lifting the entire compact section. Here, there is room for some small items, money, a hanky, and other trinkets.

Whiting & Davis manufactured the rare, compact-topped Dresden and Ivorytone armor mesh purses. The Ivorytone is an armor mesh purse that has an unusual color scheme. The Dresden is colored ring mesh. The compacts on these frames are round and the attached mesh purses are vivid in color. Compacts can be found centered on the frame or off to the side. Linings could be ordered in a bevy of pretty pastel colors. The bags are spacious, with a beveled glass mirror attached to a silk lining with a reinforced silk tab. One style in particular, called The Swinging Compact Costume Bag contains the compact centered in the frame, but instead of sitting rigidly in its place, the compact swings on a hinge. This is a very difficult piece to find; it was expensive originally and can command a hefty price again today.

The R & G Company is the most elusive of all the major manufacturers of vanity purses for nothing is known about them. An R & G Company made corsets in the late nineteenth century, but it is not known if this company has any connection with these purses. The R & G purses that exist are of high quality with compact tops of very intricately enameled flowers and foliage in pastel colors on sterling silver. Sturdy wrist straps are made from a tightly woven braid or foxtail mesh. Inside, a round compact section has a mirror and a large receptacle for packed powder. Below the metal powder container is a spacious mesh bag. The metal bands around the outside of the compact are etched in silver flowers. Elaborately enameled or plain armor mesh purses by R & G were available in regular link sizes as well as the finer quality baby flat mesh. The bags are embellished with metal chain tassels.

The Evans Case Company also produced a mesh vanity purse. Incorporated in 1922 in North Attleboro, Massachusetts, the Evans name is more famous for cigarette lighters and other novelties. Their most popular vanity bag has a round, gold plated or enameled compact top and a flat mesh goldtone body. One style is oval with enameling on the compact lid. Linings are silk, usually in an ivory color. Whiting & Davis supplied the mesh for Evans, but Evans did not produce nearly the quantity of vanity bags that Whiting & Davis did. The Evans Company also made special vanity bags for sororities and clubs with identifying insignia enameled or stamped onto the frame. Carry chains were made of link or foxtail mesh and some had finger ring attachments.

The "Du Barry Bag" was introduced through this formal announcement in *The Jeweler's Circular* trade magazine. An innovative design required unconventionally attaching the compact to the carry strap instead of the purse frame. *Courtesy of The Napier Company archives*

The *Delysia* was manufactured by Whiting and Davis in the 1920s, in standard, junior and petite sizes. 2x4. *From the Collection of Paula Higgins*

A rare early plastic bolster shaped compact purse. 2 1/2x5. *From the Collection of Joyce Morgan, Photograph by Harry Barth*

"For her and her daughter." The *Delysia* and the *Baby Peggy*. *Cosmopolitan, December, 1924*

Shown open it displays the compact nestled in the center of the bag. 2x4 *From the Collection of Paula Higgins*

The *Delysia* is difficult to find in fine mesh. 3x6. *From the Collection of Joyce Morgan, Photograph by Harry Barth*

Sterling silver bolster shaped *necessaire* that houses a compact inside the lid. 1 3/4x4. *From the Collection of Joyce Morgan, Photograph by Harry Barth*

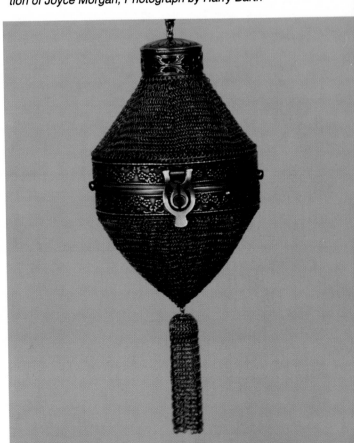

130

The Ladies Home Journal, October, 1924

A trade advertisement for The Whiting and Davis bag, the *New Piccadilly* with a "loose–pact" and "rouge–pact." *Courtesy of The Napier Company archives*

3x6. *From the Collection of Joyce Morgan, Photograph by Harry Barth*

The *Piccadilly* was a popular vanity bag in the 1920s. *The Saturday Evening Post, September, 1922*

The *El–Sah* vanity bag with a fancy enameled floral lid. 3 1/2x7 1/2. *From the Collection of Joyce Morgan, Photograph by Harry Barth*

From the Collection of Joyce Morgan, Photograph by Harry Barth

The R & G Company vanity bag with sterling enameled lid and finely crafted foxtail wrist strap. Notice the high quality embossing around the metal bands containing the compact. 2 1/2x7. *From the Collection of Joyce Morgan, Photograph by Harry Barth*

Left: an El–Sah displayed open reveals powder and rouge pots, oval mirror and comb holder, right shows a rare jeweled and enamel encrusted version. *Author's Collection, Photograph by Dan Civitello*

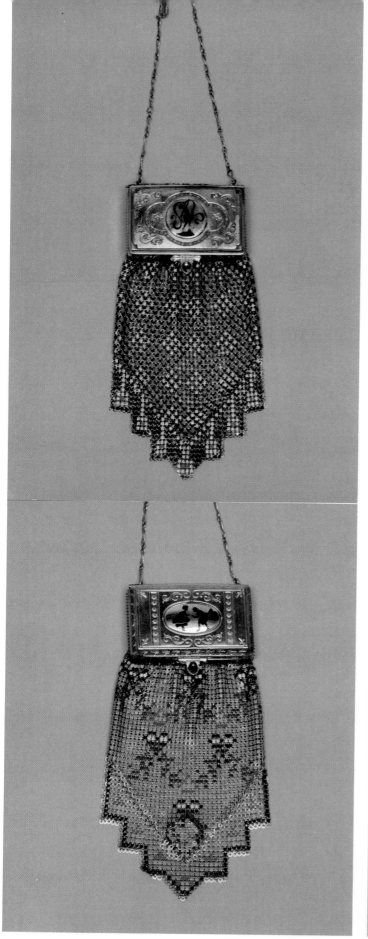

This vanity bag by The R & G Company has baby mesh with a sterling enameled lid and mesh tassel. 2 1/2x7. *From the Collection of Joyce Morgan, Photograph by Harry Barth*

A popular Whiting and Davis design with silhouetted figures in a dance pose on the compact lid. *From the Collection of Joyce Morgan, Photograph by Harry Barth*

The Evans Company Scotty dog motif vanity bag with lipstick attached via a tango chain. 3x5. *The Curiosity Shop, Photograph by Walter Kitik*

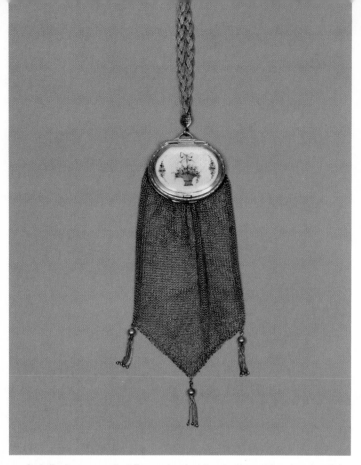

A delicate enameled flower basket in sterling with a lovely triple tasseled finish. 3x7. *From the Collection of Joyce Morgan, Photograph by Harry Barth*

In the tradition of a trinity plated compact is this distinctly unusual purse with a compact located on the front. 3 1/4x4. *From the Collection of Joyce Morgan, Photograph by Harry Barth*

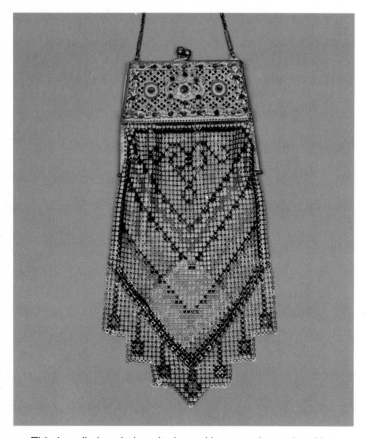

This heavily jeweled vanity bag with unusual crosshatching on the compact lid is by Whiting and Davis. 4x9. *From the Collection of Joyce Morgan, Photograph by Harry Barth*

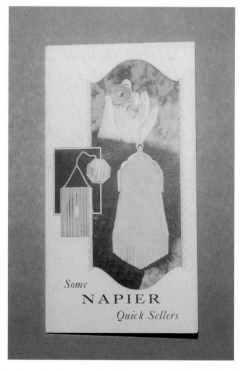

Napier trade advertisement. *Courtesy of The Napier Company archives*

A note found on the inside of this lovely rare vanity bag reads: "My evening bag from Jaccards from Jake–1925." 3 1/4x4 1/2. *From the Collection of Joyce Morgan, Photograph by Harry Barth*

The Ladies Home Journal, November, 1922

An accordion style (gate top) compact purse frame shown open. *The Curiosity Shop, Photograph by Walter Kitik*

The R & G Company sterling enameled compact top. 2 1/2x7. *From the Collection of Joyce Morgan, Photograph by Harry Barth*

Dance Purses

Dance purses are distinctively fancy, dainty, appealing, and often found with glass jewels and intricate embellishments pressed in brass. Considered fashionable novelty items of the early twentieth century, they were created in a variety of designs and shapes including: horseshoe, trapezoid, rectangle, and oval. The most desirable dance purses are those adorned with ornate metal tassels and carry chains decorated with glass jewels. Sometimes marked "Trinity Plate," they are cousins to the similarly stamped, jewel encrusted, ladies' compacts popular in that era. Inside most dance purses, you will find a silk lining with one or two sheared pockets for hankies, tickets or paper money. Small beveled glass mirrors that could slip in and out of the pocket are attached to a fine metal chain.

Barely large enough to carry even the smallest of necessities, the dance purse was elegantly draped over the arm at a formal dance function, designed to complete the fashion statement. Difficult to find today, they are often collected in combination with other antique purses. The charm of their novel shapes and small sizes, combined with pretty ornamentation, makes it easy to see why they are favorites among most collectors.

Griffins guard the ball and socket entrance to this unique emerald green velvet dance bag. Traces of enameling are found on the ornate faux emerald and pearl studded frame. The original braided gold metal chain tassel hangs from the bottom of this triangular shaped purse. The interior is of beige silk taffeta with pockets and braid trim, mid- to late nineteenth century, European. 4x5. *From the Collection of Paula Higgins*

A reverse painted butterfly hovers over flowers on a glass front dance bag. Jeweled gilded brass adorns this rectangular shaped novelty. Filigree and openwork metal surrounds the ball and socket closure. Inside is a mirror and silk pouch lining. Late nineteenth century. 2 1/2x3 3/4. *From the Collection of Joyce Morgan, Photograph by Harry Barth*

136

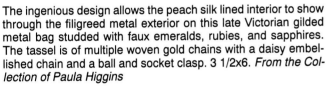

The ingenious design allows the peach silk lined interior to show through the filigreed metal exterior on this late Victorian gilded metal bag studded with faux emeralds, rubies, and sapphires. The tassel is of multiple woven gold chains with a daisy embellished chain and a ball and socket clasp. 3 1/2x6. *From the Collection of Paula Higgins*

Fascinating shapes incorporated with unusual designs are telltale characteristics of the elusive dance bag, and these are the traits that set it apart from other purses. Filigree, flowers and faux jewels define the qualities of this highly uncommon shaped novelty item. 2 1/2x3 1/2. *From the Collection of Joyce Morgan, Photograph by Harry Barth*

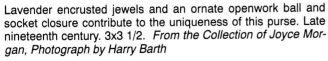

Lavender encrusted jewels and an ornate openwork ball and socket closure contribute to the uniqueness of this purse. Late nineteenth century. 3x3 1/2. *From the Collection of Joyce Morgan, Photograph by Harry Barth*

Small shapes, decorative forms, and simple convenience are attributes of the collectible dance purse. 2 3/4x4 3/4. *From the Collection of Joyce Morgan, Photograph by Harry Barth*

137

Rarities & Curiosities

Unorthodox materials, unique designs, and the degree of difficulty used in construction are key factors used to determine the value of the extraordinary purses featured in this chapter. Not as easily labeled as other rare and unusual purses featured in this book, these novel purses are also conversation pieces. Deserving a category all their own they include: fine glass beaded florals uniquely combined with scenic petitpoint inserts, purses made of unusual mediums like etched and naturally dyed shell, the application of curious materials like watermelon seeds fashioned into a usable purse, an exquisitely painted porcelain masterpiece, and a purse that incorporates a watch as part of the frame that was difficult and expensive to manufacture.

A rose colored, watered silk lining protects the interior. *From the Collection of Paula Higgins*

Few purses stand in categories by themselves like this double sided mother of pearl porcelain figural masterpiece. Trimmed in red leather, it features a centrally located hand painted medallion of two young women in a pastoral scene, framed in engraved sterling with a simple push button clasp. No markings are found on the European origin purse that can be dated to the early or mid-nineteenth century. 2 1/2x3. *From the Collection of Paula Higgins*

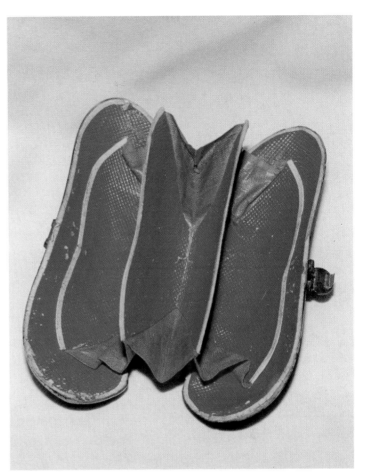

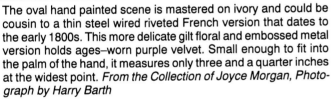

A heavy, red, textured, three sectional paper is revealed as the shell carved purse is shown open. The center section was used for coin. *From the Collection of Paula Higgins*

The oval hand painted scene is mastered on ivory and could be cousin to a thin steel wired riveted French version that dates to the early 1800s. This more delicate gilt floral and embossed metal version holds ages–worn purple velvet. Small enough to fit into the palm of the hand, it measures only three and a quarter inches at the widest point. *From the Collection of Joyce Morgan, Photograph by Harry Barth*

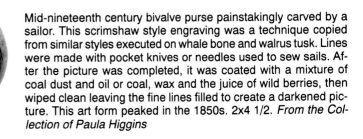

Mid-nineteenth century bivalve purse painstakingly carved by a sailor. This scrimshaw style engraving was a technique copied from similar styles executed on whale bone and walrus tusk. Lines were made with pocket knives or needles used to sew sails. After the picture was completed, it was coated with a mixture of coal dust and oil or coal, wax and the juice of wild berries, then wiped clean leaving the fine lines filled to create a darkened picture. This art form peaked in the 1850s. 2x4 1/2. *From the Collection of Paula Higgins*

A strong Art Nouveau influence is depicted in the swirling silver metal adorning this rare watch purse. Made of black leather, it houses a watch centrally located as an ornamental part of the rigid encasement. 2 1/4" diameter. *From the Collection of Joyce Morgan, Photograph by Harry Barth*

A watermelon seed reticule style bag with cut steel beads netted over black silk. Notice the extra care used in the amalgamation of two unorthodox mediums: seed and steel beads, as fringe and ball tassel adornments. Pink silk lining, early twentieth century. 7 1/2x14. *From the Collection of Paula Higgins*

An unconventional combination incorporates a petitpoint insert with fine glass beads creating a scarce purse. Petitpoint scenes are present on both sides of the bag, but are rarely of the same subject matter. Made in Austria, ca. 1900. Approximate size: 7x10. *From the Collection of Joyce Morgan, Photograph by Walter Kitik*

Children's Purses

Dainty celluloid children's purses were made in the early twentieth century, but because this form of plastic was light weight and fragile, few are found today in good repair. Ironically, the very facts of celluloid's unstable nature and short manufacturing period contribute to the present high value for existing examples.

In the 1930s, thousands of "kiddy" mesh bags were produced by The Whiting & Davis Company. Since they were much smaller than the adult versions of enameled mesh bags, they were less expensive to manufacture. Parents could easily afford to buy an authentic Whiting & Davis mesh bag for their daughters which gave the youngsters an opportunity to accessorize just like their mothers. A child's bag featuring Mickey and Minnie Mouse enameled onto the frame sold for one dollar. Since many children did not take care of the bags, most were lost or damaged beyond repair and thrown away. The few that can be found today are usually not in good condition, but collectors regard them as valuable keepsakes.

A dainty celluloid egg shaped vanity purse with applied painted flowers and matching celluloid finger ring. Early twentieth century. 2x3. *Author's Collection, Photograph by Walter Kitik*

"Mickey and Minnie Mouse" are embossed and enameled on the frame of this children's Whiting and Davis ring mesh bag. 2 1/2x3 1/2. *Author's Collection, Photograph by Walter Kitik*

"The three little pigs" dangle charmingly off the frame of this children's Whiting and Davis enameled ring mesh purse. 2 1/2x3 1/2. *From the Collection of Joyce Morgan, Photograph by Harry Barth*

Montgomery Ward, 1932

A Whiting and Davis enameled flat link mesh bag with an enameled pendant drop of a gilded bird. It has the original shield shaped tag and was a more expensive children's purse. 2 1/4x4 1/2. *From the Collection of Joyce Morgan, Photograph by Harry Barth*

An interesting combination of children's purses; the larger fabric bag has a silk trimmed painted cartoon style face affixed to its front and is pictured with two unique celluloid coin purses. The coin purses have a round lid that is slid over a carry cord in order to gain access to the interior. Applied on the lids are a witch on a broom and a bunny with a carrot. Also pictured is a mirror with a painted silk face that was found in the fabric bag. *The Curiosity Shop, Photograph by Dan Civitello*

Whiting and Davis targeted their advertisements to include mothers as well as daughters. *Cosmopolitan, December 1924*

The Home Purse-Making Market

From the mid-nineteenth century onward, people were encouraged to make their own purses by advertisements for the supplies in many popular journals of the day. Easy to follow and intricate patterns, sponsored by bead manufacturers, silk twist and yarn companies, purse frame suppliers and trading companies, could be found in magazines, books and newspapers. One promoter, The Brainerd & Armstrong Company (established in 1867 in New London, Connecticut), offered purse-making as a convenient and practical way to become a home artisan. By the turn of the century, this company was one of the leaders in publishing embroidery lessons and instructions for knitting and crocheting silk bags and purses. Designs had to be clearly written by competent workers who experimented and created new designs, literally making the bags prior to publication. To prove out the design, these books utilized color plates. A corps of expert embroiderers and bag makers edited the finished manuscript before it was presented for purchase. The return of empty filo & floss silk holders helped to lessen the cost of the manual. Bags could be made both with and without the use of beads.

Sample cards were sold to at-home beaded bag makers, demonstrating floss, embroidery and crochet silk thread dyed in appealing shades. Instructions encouraged the use of their crochet silk, purse twists and sewing silk. The knitting silk thread, claimed to be the longest, strongest, smoothest and "to excel above others in terms of evenness, shade and wearing qualities," cost $.35 per spool, a sizable amount at the time when crochet silk sold for $.25, and the least expensive sewing silk cost $.10. Thread was sold to retail storekeepers and thus made available to the public in 50- and 100-yard lengths. Other items necessary to bag making, such as steel metal beads priced at $.12 per "bunch" and crochet hooks at $.05 each, were listed. Products were not available everywhere, and merchandise, if not found on local storekeepers' shelves, was offered directly from the company. However, by 1901, purse-making essentials could be found with more convenience by selling agents in many large cities including Chicago, Illinois; St. Paul, Minnesota; St. Louis, Missouri; Cincinnati, Ohio; San Francisco, California; and St. Johns, Canada. An excerpt from the instructions on how a round, bottom-beaded, crocheted purse was to be made read as follows:

String a large number of the beads at a time so as not to make the cutting of the silk necessary very often. When it becomes necessary, do it this way: cut the silk half an inch from the crochet needle, then pull out of the crochet just enough of the thread to enable you to tie a knot, being careful not to drop any beads. The half inch is allowed for the knot. When you have your beads strung and fastened this way, you can easily crochet over the knot without any trouble, for then you have the exact number of beads before the knot. The knot is of course pulled toward the inside. Begin on the bottom of the purse with 25 chain stitches. Into the second chain work a single chain without a bead for an increase. Now, on each stitch to the end, work a plain single chain, then one with bead. In the last stitch work three, and, on opposite side of chain, alternate also with plain and beaded single chain. At the end make an extra one in with bead, where the two are already worked in, then join on top of the first plain single chain. This makes 28 stitches in the round, four of which were increases.

The beaded shopping bag was made with purse twist thread and six bunches of steel beads. Shown with a detailed purse frame that was sewn on to the body of the bag and attached to a chatelaine hook, it could easily slide over a belt. It was not a large purse as the name might imply, but rather a convenient carrier of money and small items that could be taken on a shopping excursion. Since the user's hands were left free, a lady could browse in comfort. The fringe instructions for the beaded shopping bag were relatively simple:

Finish the bottom of the purse with three vandykes in steel beads with fringe. Use 11 beads for the loops to make the vandykes and 39 beads for the fringe.

A beaded gate-top purse required one spool of purse twist, three bunches of steel beads, and a gate-top frame. Twisted loop fringe instructions for the gate-top are as follows:

Finish the bottom with graduated fringe. Begin with 10 beads, increase by fives to 45, then down to 10, and each time, before sewing the fringe fast, bring it up through the preceding one, which gives the twist between the fringes.

An odd looking, long black spectacle case with steel beads called for one spool of black crochet silk, three bunches of steel beads, one steel clasp (frame) and a number four crochet needle. Pictured attached to a chatelaine hook, it was finished with a beaded tassel affixed to a rounded bottom. The tassel consisted of eight strands with fifty steel beads on each. A black bag with steel beads, which had a pull top drawn through with a ribbon commanded two spools of black crochet silk, eight bunches of steel beads, three to eight yards of silk, one steel frame, and a number four crochet needle. Instructions, as they appeared in 1902, on how to make beaded fringe for the black steel beaded bag mentioned above suggested:

1st row– String 5 beads on a needle full of silk; begin 1/2 inch up side of bag; catch every 4th st round to other side.

2d row– Slip needle through 2 first bds in loop of 5 in first row, string 5 bds, catch into 3d bd in loop in first row, repeat to end. 3d row– Same as 2d.

4th row– String 50 bds, catch into middle bead in 3d row of loops, twist in and out twice, fasten to next loop, repeat round.

In the 1920s, "new" beaded bags were introduced to the American public. Taken for granted that homemakers were the target market, manuals with step-by-step instructions could conveniently be purchased in specialty shops or by mail. One could afford the latest edition which sold for only ten cents and included patterns to make over ten bags. Illustrations with fashionable ladies of the era holding alluring purses and jewelry would grace the covers. Simplicity of design and a refined appearance were promised as practical patterns and handy bead charts along with encouraging photographs of completed purses were included. Purse assemblers could easily find bead selecting tips and other sound advice. Guides were peppered with advertisements describing their products and assuring perfect results in making bags. People had to remember to order enough thread and beads at the onset so as not to run short before completing the project. Dyes had a tendency to vary slightly in color from one lot to the next and since beads were imported, there could be no guarantee that additional materials would match or be accessible at any given time. A wide range of products available included: filigree and early plastic purse frames with carry chains, yarn, pure silk thread, steel crochet hooks, and knitting and sewing needles.

Most of these bag patterns required crocheting or knitting, along with beading as part of the process, and each bag was supplied with a name and a corresponding invoice number. The novice could choose from a special selection of illustrated purses that could be made by "ordinary sewing." The firms offering these booklets were based in New York. Dritz–Traum were distributors of Hiawatha beads, frames, bead silk and bead needle sets. Julroberts also sold beads, crochet hooks, frames, purse twist and other products. The Hemingway Silk Company produced Hemingway Silks and owned mills in the quaint towns of Putnam, Watertown, and Woodbury, all located in Connecticut.

Bead craft catalogs were essential to home artisans. N.E. Johns & Company from Cincinnati, Ohio offered a large black and white illustrated directory presenting numerous materials, accessories, and instructions used in bag making. An extensive selection of purse frames and various carry chains were displayed along with canvas patterns, stamped in color, used to sew exceptional needlepoint bags or provide a foundation for beaded bags. Adornments consisted of beads, rhinestones, powder puff cases and handbag mirrors. Miscellaneous items such as elastic, braided silk cord, loom needles, waxed bead silk, foxtail and other necessities were also presented. Beads were imported Venetian, French Limoges, jet, coral, bone, amber, ivory, and crystal. For the avid purse maker, other published beadwork books were listed with a description of their contents and the cost that varied from five to twenty–five cents each. Each of these American-home-made beaded bags was truly beautiful and unique.

By the 1930s, the era of The Great Depression, people were given yet another way to fashion these time-consuming and fragile objects. "A highly practical craft of superb interest" was reintroduced in 1937. Called "wood bead craft" and offered by Walco Bead Company, it was a great time saver resulting in colorful bags. Hours were saved in making this type of bag and hobbyists were able to make accessories with remaining beads. Not only was it quick and easy, but it also provided an excellent opportunity for organizations to support petty cash accounts and raise money for charity. Beads were highly polished and made of selected hard, close–grained woods. They were stained in an array of attractive colors and guaranteed not to fade even when wet.

Holes in the beads were large and easily manipulated with a blunt–end needle. Soon, craft instructors in schools, camps, and girls' and boys' organizations were teaching the new hobby and many young people made belts, necklaces, bracelets and other costume jewelry as well as bags. The new hobby fulfilled demand, but results were not of the caliber or collectibility of their earlier counterparts.

In the 1940s, products of the Bernhard Ulmann Co. Inc., offering their Bucilla line, and the Heirloom Needlework Guild, Inc., which now distributed Hiawatha products, were found in arts and craft shops. Booklets showed matching collar, cuff, belt, and purse sets in the latest styles. Instead of illustrations, stylish models were photographed wearing these ensembles. In 1943, hat, bag, belt and accessory patterns were offered by Bucilla. Items were crocheted with Straw–craft and Straw–twist made of Rayon. Inventory numbers of products were conveniently listed within patterns to provide easy reference when ordering. In 1945, Wonoco Yarn Company of New York offered a booklet that sold for $.20 showing bag fashions made by Corde and Corde–twist. The bags were crocheted and had names such as Debonair, Roulette, and Sunburst. They were beadless with Lucite handles twisted and curved into fancy shapes. The Jack Frost Yarn Company and Peter Pan also offered matching crocheted hat and bag pattern books. Metal and early plastic purse frames were seldom used and zippered closures with handmade beaded straps took precedent. Bags were started with foundations, in shapes of octagons, squares, and rectangles. Purses now took on a drastically different look from their counterparts back in the Twenties and Thirties. Consequently, the inclination to make those extraordinary bags had abruptly changed, from a captivating skill, to a quick and easy craft. Sadly, the tendency to make those marvelous purses was rapidly becoming a dying pastime.

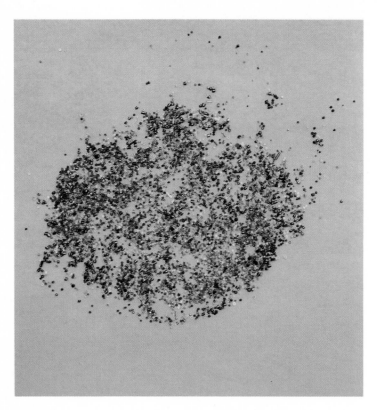

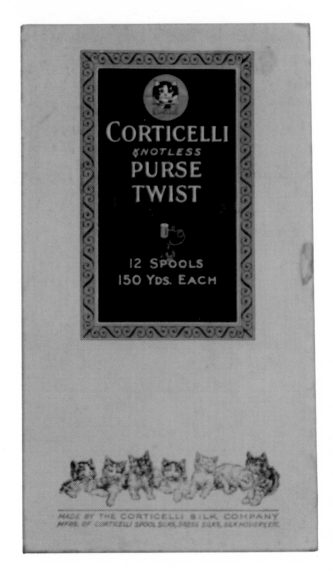

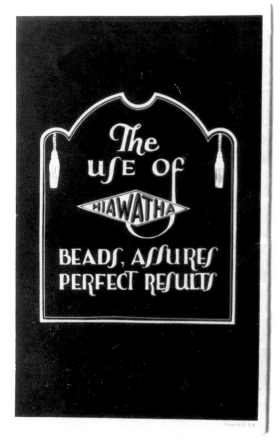

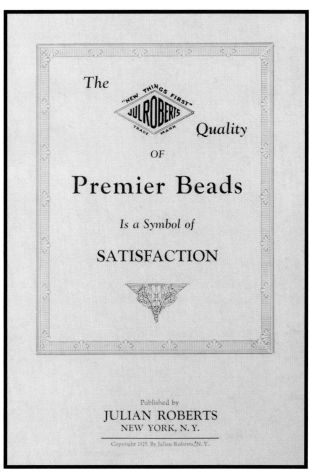

HEMINWAY SILKS

*The Standard of Quality
for Seventy - five Years*

Sample card advertisement. *The Brainerd and Armstrong Company*

ROUND BOTTOM BEADED PURSE.

The round bottom beaded purse. *The Brainerd and Armstrong Company*

The beaded shopping bag. *The Brainerd and Armstrong Company*

The beaded gate top purse has a frame that is also referred to as accordion style. *The Brainerd and Armstrong Company*

The peculiar looking spectacle case. *The Brainerd and Armstrong Company*

Booklets with beaded bag instructions sold for ten cents in the 1920s.

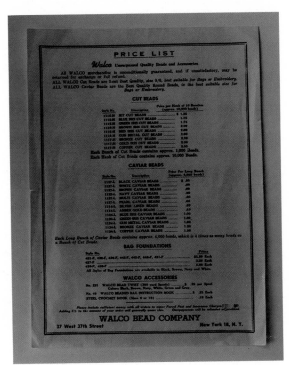

Bead price list.

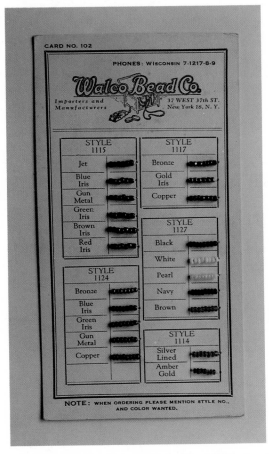

A glass beaded sample card issued by The Walco Bead Company.

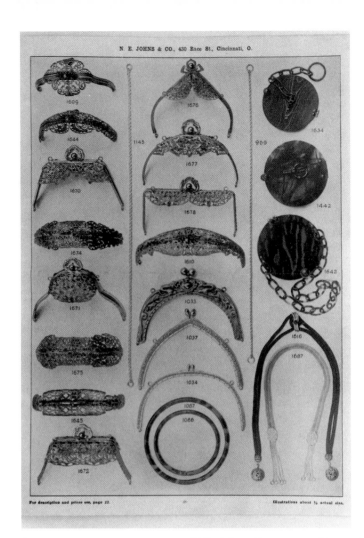

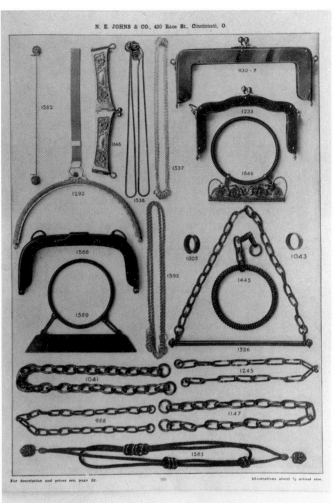

N.E. Johns Company sold a variety of beautiful purse frames.
Beadcraft, The Art Beautiful

Canvas patterns were stamped in color and could be ordered
through a catalog by N.E. Johns Company, ca. 1930s. *Beadcraft,
The Art Beautiful*

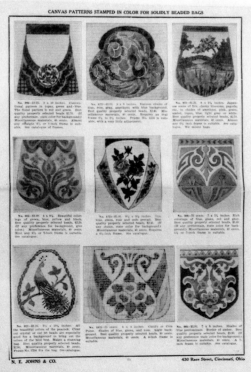

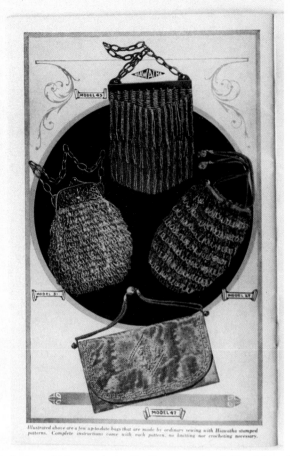

Bags that could be made by "ordinary sewing." *The Hiawatha Book*

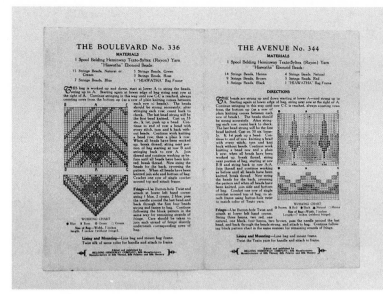

Patterns and instructions for two beaded bags.

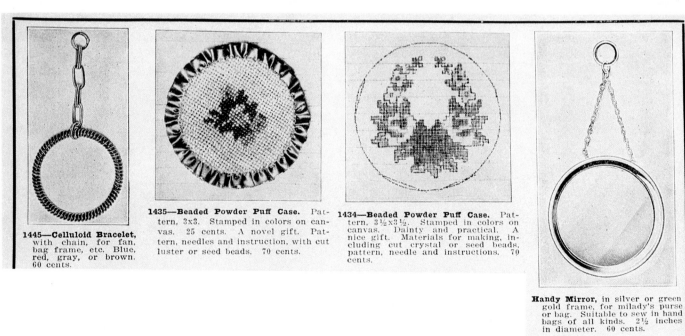

An interesting assortment of purse adornments were sold through catalogs for the beadworker. *Beadcraft, The Art Beautiful*

The
Avenue
No. 344

BELDING HEMINWAY
Texto~Syltex
~RAYON~
YARN

The chic of the new
mode is truly express-
ed by The Avenue
handbag. Made up by
you this bag will cost
approximately $5.85
The Avenue handbag adds that
smart touch which has come to
mean so much in the
accessories and which
at retail costs about $15

The
Boulevard
No. 336

BELDING HEMINWAY
Texto~Syltex
~RAYON~
YARN

The Boulevard hand
bag can be made for
the surprisingly small
cost of $5.50
Individuality is the key note of
the new mode. Individuality the
key note set by the Boulevard.
Average retail cost of
this bag approximate-
ly $15

The Avenue and *The Boulevard.*

Get acquainted with all our fascinating crafts.

Send for the following instruction and design booklets with sample cards and price lists:

INDIAN BEADCRAFT Instruction and Design Pamphlet and
Sample Card of Indian Seed Beads .... $ .25 per Set

WOOD BEADCRAFT Instruction and Design Booklet No. 21 and
Sample Card of Wood Beads .... .25 per Set

TILE CRAFT Instruction and Design Booklet No. 10 and Sample
Card of Tile Craft Beads .... .25 per Set

CUBE BEAD CRAFT Instruction and Design Booklet No. 18 and
Sample Card of Cube Wood Beads .... .25 per Set

SEQUIN CRAFT Instruction Pamphlet and Sample Card of Sequins   .25 per Set

CROCHET BEADED BAG Instruction and Design Booklet No. 49
and Sample Card of Beads .... .25 per Set

WALCO BEAD COMPANY, 37 West 37th Street, New York 18, N. Y.

Advertisement sheet for wood beads. *Walco Bead Company*

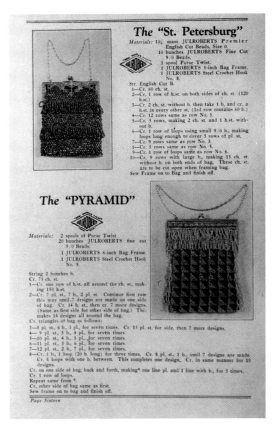

Instructions for *The St. Petersburg* and *The Pyramid. JulRoberts*

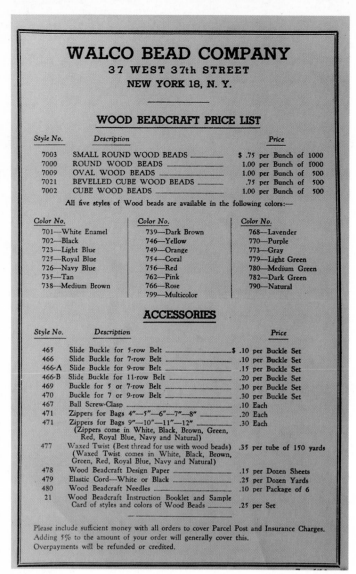

WALCO BEAD COMPANY
37 WEST 37th STREET
NEW YORK 18, N. Y.

WOOD BEADCRAFT PRICE LIST

Style No.	Description	Price
7003	SMALL ROUND WOOD BEADS	$ .75 per Bunch of 1000
7000	ROUND WOOD BEADS	1.00 per Bunch of 1000
7009	OVAL WOOD BEADS	1.00 per Bunch of 500
7021	BEVELLED CUBE WOOD BEADS	.75 per Bunch of 500
7002	CUBE WOOD BEADS	1.00 per Bunch of 500

All five styles of Wood beads are available in the following colors:—

Color No.	Color No.	Color No.
701—White Enamel	739—Dark Brown	768—Lavender
702—Black	746—Yellow	770—Purple
723—Light Blue	749—Orange	773—Gray
725—Royal Blue	754—Coral	779—Light Green
726—Navy Blue	756—Red	780—Medium Green
735—Tan	762—Pink	782—Dark Green
738—Medium Brown	766—Rose	790—Natural
	799—Multicolor	

ACCESSORIES

Style No.	Description	Price
465	Slide Buckle for 5-row Belt	$ .10 per Buckle Set
466	Slide Buckle for 7-row Belt	.10 per Buckle Set
466-A	Slide Buckle for 9-row Belt	.15 per Buckle Set
466-B	Slide Buckle for 11-row Belt	.20 per Buckle Set
469	Buckle for 5 or 7-row Belt	.30 per Buckle Set
470	Buckle for 7 or 9-row Belt	.30 per Buckle Set
467	Ball Screw-Clasp	.10 Each
471	Zippers for Bags 4"—5"—6"—7"—8"	.20 Each
471	Zippers for Bags 9"—10"—11"—12"	.30 Each
	(Zippers come in White, Black, Brown, Green, Red, Royal Blue, Navy and Natural)	
477	Waxed Twist (Best thread for use with wood beads) (Waxed Twist comes in White, Black, Brown, Green, Red, Royal Blue, Navy and Natural)	.35 per tube of 150 yards
478	Wood Beadcraft Design Paper	.15 per Dozen Sheets
479	Elastic Cord—White or Black	.25 per Dozen Yards
480	Wood Beadcraft Needles	.10 per Package of 6
21	Wood Beadcraft Instruction Booklet and Sample Card of styles and colors of Wood Beads	.25 per Set

Please include sufficient money with all orders to cover Parcel Post and Insurance Charges. Adding 5% to the amount of your order will generally cover this. Overpayments will be refunded or credited.

Wood beadcraft and accessory price list. *Walco Bead Company*

Colorful wood beads shown on a sample card. *Walco Bead Company*

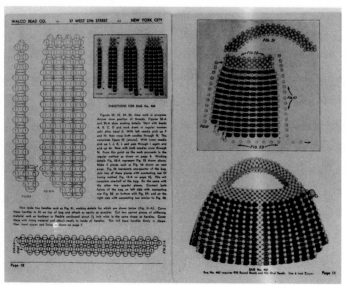

Pattern and instructions for a wood bead crafted bag. *Walco Bead Company*

A wood bead crafted purse with zipper closure shown with loose wooden beads. *The Curiosity Shop, Photograph by Walter Kitik*

Bibliography

Baker, Lillian *Art Nouveau and Art Deco Jewelry, Identification and Value Guide*, Paducah, Kentucky, Collector Books, 1981.

Barbour, Emma Post, *New Bead Book,* Chicago, National Trading Company, 1924.

Bead Craft, The Art Beautiful, No. 25, 27 & 28, Cincinnati, Ohio, N.E. Johns & Co. Inc., 1934.

Bell Jeanenne, *Answers to Questions about Old Jewelry,* 3rd ed. Florence, Alabama, Books Americana, 1992.

Book of Bags, A, New York, New York, The H.K.H. Silk Co. Inc., 1922.

Book of Bags, The, No. 3, New York, New York, The H.K.H. Silk Company, no date.

Bucilla Strawcraft, New York, New York, Bernhard Ulmann Co. Inc., 1943.

Davidov, Corinne & Ginny Redington Dawes, *The Bakelite Jewelry Book,* New York, New York, Abbeville Press, 1988.

Embroidery Lessons with Colored Studies, New London, Connecticut, The Brainerd & Armstrong Co., 1901.

Feild, Rachael, *Collectors Style Guide Victoriana,* New York, New York, Ballantine Books, 1989.

Few Bags, A, New York, New York, The H.K.H. Silk Co. Inc., no date.

Haertig, Evelyn, *More Beautiful Purses,* Carmel, California, Gallery Graphics Press, 1981.

Hiawatha Book, The; How to Make the New Beaded Bags and Chains, Ed. VII, New York, New York, Dritz-Traum Co., 1924.

Jack Frost Handbags, Vol. 48, New York, New York, Gottlieb Bros., 1944.

Kelly, Lyngerda & Nancy Schiffer, *Plastic Jewelry,* Atglen, Pennsylvania, Schiffer Publishing Ltd., 1987.

Metropolitan Museum of Art, The, *Treasures of Tutankhamun,* 4th printing, New York, Ballantine Books, 1978.

Miller, Harrice Simons, *Official Identification and Price Guide to Costume Jewelry,* New York, New York, House of Collectibles, 1990.

New Simplified Instructions for Making Crocheted and Knitted Beaded Bags and Chains of Exclusive Design, New York, New York, Julian Roberts, Inc., 1925.

New Simplified Instructions for Making Crocheted and Knitted Beaded Bags and Attractive Gifts, 4th ed., New York, New York, Julian Roberts, Inc., 1927.

New Hand-Crochet Fashions by Dritz, Vol. 27, New York, New York, John Dritz & Co., 1945.

Summertime Loveliness, New York, New York, The Belding Hemingway Company, no date.

Walco Beaded Bags, No. 49, New York, New York, Walco Bead Co., Inc. 1948.

Wonoco Bag Fashions, Corde and Corde-Twist, New York, New York, Wonoco Yarn Company, no date.

Wood Bead Craft, New York, New York, Walco Bead Co. Importers, 1937.

Price Guide

Prices vary immensely according to the condition of the piece, the location of the market, and the overall quality of the design and manufacture. Condition is always of paramount importance in assigning a value. Prices in the Midwest differ from those in the West or East, and those at specialty antique shows will vary from those at general shows. And, of course, being at the right place at the right time can make all the difference.

All these factors make it impossible to create an absolutely accurate price list, but we can offer a guide. The prices reflect what one could realistically expect to pay at retail or auction.

The left hand number is the page number. The letters following it indicate the position of the photograph on the page: T=top, L=left, R=right, TL=top left, TR=top right, C=center, CL=center left, CR=center right, B=bottom, BL=bottom left, and BR=bottom right. The right hand column of numbers are the estimated price ranges in United States dollars.

Page	Pos	Price	Page	Pos	Price	Page	Pos	Price
5	L	R	20	BL	R	34	BR	100–175
5	R	300–400	20	BR	295–395	37	BL	R
6	TL	250–350	21	TL	R	37	BR	R
6	TR	250–350	21	BL	R	38	TL	150–250
6	BL	250–350	21	BR	VR	38	TR	200–300
6	BR	R	22	TL	300–400	38	BL	200–300
7	TL	250–350	22	TR	VR	38	BR	200–300
7	TR	175–275	22	BL	R	39	TL	150–250
7	BL	R	23	TL	R	39	TR	175–275
7	BR	150–250	23	TR	275–375	39	BL	125–175
8	TL	275–375R	23	BL	150–250	39	BR	150–250
8	TR	VR	23	BR	R	40	TL	50–125
8	BL	R	24	L	200–275	40	TR	125–225
8	BR	275–375R	24	TR	VR	40	BL	125–225
9	TL	R	24	BR	300–400	40	BR	225–325
9	TR	150–225	25	TL	VR	42	L	VR
9	BL	275–375	25	R	250–350	42	R	R
10	TL	250–350	26	TL	125–200	45	TL	275–375
10	TR	150–250	26	TR	125–175	45	TR	175–275
10	BL	175–275	26	BL	225–275R	45	BR	R
10	BR	R	27	TL	75–125	46	TR	125–175
11	TL	150–250	27	TR	125–200	46	BL	50–125
11	TR	75–125	27	BL	200–300	46	BR	R
11	BL	125–175	28	TL	150–250	47	FRAMES	50–150
11	BR	275–375	28	TR	175–275	47	PURSE	75–150
12	TL	VR	28	BL	150–250	48	TL	R
12	TR	125–175	28	BR	175–275	48	BL	175–275
12	BL	R	29	TL	150–250	48	BR	275–375
13	TL	150–200	29	TR	175–275	49	TL	VR
13	TR	125–250	29	BL	150–250	49	TR	275–375
13	BL	150–200	29	BR	95–145	49	BL	VR
13	BR	125–150	30	TL	75–125	49	BR	300–400
14	TL	75–125	30	TR	100–175	50	L	R
14	TR	75–125	30	BL	175–275	50	TR	300–400
14	BL	75–100	30	BR	125–175	50	BR	175–275
14	BR	75–150	31	L	200–300R	51	TL	VR
16	TR	50–100	31	BR	75–125	51	TR	225–325
18	B	75–155	32	TL	225–325	51	BL	VR
19	TL	VR	33	TL	R	52	TL	VR
19	TR	VR	33	TR	175–275	52	TR	275–375
19	BL	VR	33	BL	VR	52	BL	275–375
19	BR	VR	33	BR	150–250	52	BR	175–275
20	TL	295–395	34	TL	175–275	54	TL	225–325
20	TR	VR	34	TR	R	54	TR	75–125

No.	Loc	Price
55	TL	100–175
55	TR	125–275
55	BL	45–95
56	CR	VR
56	BL	R
70	CL	125–225
71	TR	125–225
72	TL	30–80
72	TR	150–250
72	BL	175–275
72	BR	125–225
76	TL	125–225
79	TL	125–225
79	BL	150–250
84	TL	100–200
84	TR	75–125
85	TL	75–125
85	TR	150–250
85	BL	150–250
85	BR	100–175
86	TR	75–125
86	BL	75–175
86	BR	150–250
87	TL	125–175
87	TR	150–225
87	BR	175–275
88	TR	R
88	BL	100–175
88	BR	150–250
89	TR	95–145
89	BL	R
89	BR	75–125
91	TL	65–135
91	BL	R
91	BR	R
92	TL	150–250
92	TR	R
92	BR	150–250
93	TL	VR
93	TR	125–200
93	BL	R
93	BR	75–150
94	TR	125–175
94	BR	R
95	TL	R
95	BL	75–150
95	BR	85–165
96	STAR SERIES	VR
98	BL	150–250
98	BR	150–250
99	TL	125–225
99	TR	160–260
99	BL	150–250
99	BR	150–250
100	TL	200–300
100	BL	150–250
100	BR	150–250
101	TL	R
101	TR	R
101	BL	R
101	BR	150–250
102	TL	R
102	TR	R
102	BL	VR
102	BR	75–175
103	TL	125–225
103	TR	R
103	BL	75–175
103	BR	R
104	TL	R
104	TR	125–225
104	BL	R
104	BR	75–175
105	TL	125–225
105	TR	150–250
105	BL	150–250
105	BR	150–250
106	R	R
107	BL	95–155
107	CR	VR
108	TL	175–275
108	TR	95–165
108	BL	R
108	BR	R
109	TL	150–250R
109	TR	125–225
109	BL	R
109	BR	R
110	BL	R
110	BR	VR
111	TL	150–250
111	BL	150–250
112	BL	R
112	BR	VR
113	BR	VR
114	PETITPOINT	50–150
	TAN VELVET	75–175
	PETITPOINT	50–150
	DANCE BAG	R
114	B	R
115	TL	VR
115	TR	150–250
115	BL	150–250R
115	BR	175–275
117	CARD-HOLDER	75–175
	PETITPOINT COIN	50–150
	WALLET	75–175
	PETITPOINT COIN	50–125
117	BL	150–250
117	BR	VR
118	TL	55–155
118	TR	125–225
118	PURSE	150–250
	CARD-HOLDER	50–150
118	BR	R
119	TL	R
119	TR	VR
119	BL	195–295
119	BR	95–195
120	TL	175–275
120	TR	95–195
120	TL	125–225
120	BR	R
121	TL	VR
121	BL	125–225
122	TL	150–250
122	TR	135–235
122	CL	100–200
122	BL	55–155
124	TL	150–250
124	TR	125–225
124	CL	125–225
124	BR	60–160
125	TL	125–225
125	TR	R
125	BL	100–200
126	TL	R
126	TR	125–225
126	B	75–175
129	BL	R
129	BR	R
130	TR	R
130	BL	450–550
130	BR	R
131	BL	R
132	TL	225–325
132	TR	200–300
132	BL	R
132	BR	R
133	TL	200–300
133	TR	R
133	BL	200–300
133	BR	65–125
134	TL	VR
134	TR	VR
134	BL	R
135	TL	VR
135	BL	45–95
135	BR	R
136	T	175–275R
136	B	R
137	TL	175–275R
137	TR	R
137	BL	R
137	BR	R
138	B	VR
139	TL	VR
139	B	VR
140	TL	VR
140	TR	250–350
140	BL	65–150
140	BR	250–350
141	TR	VR
141	BL	R
141	BR	R
142	TR	150–250R
142	FABRIC	75–175
142	CELLULOID	50–85
154	BR	45–75

Index